ECONOMIC ANALYSIS OF CRITICAL HABITAT DESIGNATIONS FOR 76 PLANTS FROM THE ISLANDS OF KAUA'I AND NI'IHAU

January 2001

Prepared for:

Division of Economics
U.S. Fish and Wildlife Service
4401 N. Fairfax Drive
Arlington, VA 22203

Prepared by:

Decision Analysts Hawaii, Inc.
1655 Kamole Street
Honolulu, Hawaii 96821

under subcontract to:

Industrial Economics, Incorporated
2067 Massachusetts Avenue
Cambridge, Massachusetts 02140

Send comments on the economic analysis to:

Field Supervisor
Pacific Islands Ecoregion Office
U.S. Fish and Wildlife Service
300 Ala Moana Boulevard, Room 3-122
P.O. Box 50088
Honolulu HI 96850-0001

TABLE OF CONTENTS

PREFACE

This report was prepared for the U.S. Fish and Wildlife Service (FWS) by Decision Analysts Hawaii, Inc. (DAHI), a Hawaii-based economic consulting firm, under contract to Industrial Economics, Incorporated (IEc). The report assesses the economic impacts that may result from the designation of 23 critical habitat units for 76 listed endangered and threatened species of plants on the islands of Kaua'i and Ni'ihau in the state of Hawaii.

Under Section 4(b)(1) of the 1973 Endangered Species Act (ESA), the decision to list a species as endangered or threatened is made solely on the basis of scientific data and analysis. By contrast, under Section 4(b)(2) of the ESA, the decision to designate a particular area as critical habitat must take into account the potential economic impact of the critical habitat designation. Correspondingly, this analysis addresses the potential incremental economic costs and benefits of 23 proposed critical habitat designations for the 76 species, but does not consider any economic impacts associated with the original listing of the 76 species. If the economic analysis reveals that the economic impacts of designating any area as critical habitat outweigh the benefits of designation, FWS may exclude the area from consideration, unless excluding it will result in the extinction of the species.

IEc and DAHI worked with FWS personnel, and DAHI worked with the State of Hawaii's Department of Land and Natural Resources to ensure that current and future land uses as well as potential Federal nexuses were identified appropriately. To better understand the concerns of stakeholders, FWS invited comments from the public, other concerned government agencies, the scientific community, industry, and other interested parties as to whether the court-ordered designation of critical habitat is prudent for endangered and threatened Hawaiian plant taxa in Hawaii. DAHI took these comments and suggestions into consideration in conducting its economic analysis. However, comments on the proposed rule and notice of determination of whether designation of critical habitat is prudent for Kaua'i and Ni'ihau ("the proposed Rule") had not yet been received by FWS when this economic analysis was conducted.

Also, IEc and DAHI explored with FWS officials whether any projects or programs would likely lead to (1) *adverse modification* determinations affecting any of the critical habitat units, but (2) not a *jeopardy* opinion affecting any of the listed species—a situation that can occur if a portion of a critical habitat is not occupied. The cases where this was likely to occur provided the basis for examining the more significant incremental economic impacts that would result from the 23 proposed critical habitat designations.

The following FWS terminology is *italicized* throughout the report for the benefits of readers who are unfamiliar with the terminology and want to be reminded that FWS has given specific meanings to these words and terms: *Federal involvement, Federal nexus, occupied, unoccupied, primary constituent elements,* and forms of *jeopardy* and *adverse modification.* The terms are explained in the text.

EXECUTIVE SUMMARY

Introduction

The purpose of this report is to identify and analyze the potential economic impacts that would result from the proposed designations of critical habitat units for endangered and threatened plants on the islands of Kaua'i and Ni'ihau in the state of Hawai'i. The report was prepared for the U.S. Department of the Interior's Fish and Wildlife Service (FWS) by Decision Analysts Hawaii, Inc. (DAHI), a Hawaii-based economic consulting firm, under contract to Industrial Economics, Incorporated (IEc).

Section 4(b)(2) of the Endangered Species Act (ESA) requires FWS to designate critical habitat on the basis of the best scientific data available, after taking into consideration the economic impact and any other relevant impacts of specifying an area as critical habitat. FWS may exclude an area from critical habitat designation if it determines that the benefits of excluding the area outweigh the benefits of including it unless it determines, based on the best scientific and commercial data available, that this will result in the extinction of the species.

Critical habitat designation can help focus conservation activities for a listed species by identifying areas that are essential to its conservation, and by heightening the awareness of Federal land management agencies and the public about the importance of critical habitat. In addition to its informational role, the critical habitat designation may provide protection where significant threats have been identified. This protection derives from ESA section 7, which requires Federal agencies to consult with FWS in order to ensure that activities they fund, authorize, or carry out are not likely to destroy or *adversely modify* the critical habitat.

Proposed Critical Habitat Designations

FWS has proposed that 60,636 acres be designated critical habitat for 76 endangered and threatened plant species on Kaua'i and Ni'ihau. This has been divided into 23 critical habitat units, of which 21 are on Kaua'i (60,166 acres), and two are on Ni'ihau (476 acres)—see Figure ES-1. Most of the Kaua'i units are in the interior and northwestern portions of the island on steep slopes, precipitous cliffs, valley headwalls, and other inaccessible regions having rugged topography.

Figure ES-1. Proposed Critical Habitat Units, Kaua'i and Ni'ihau

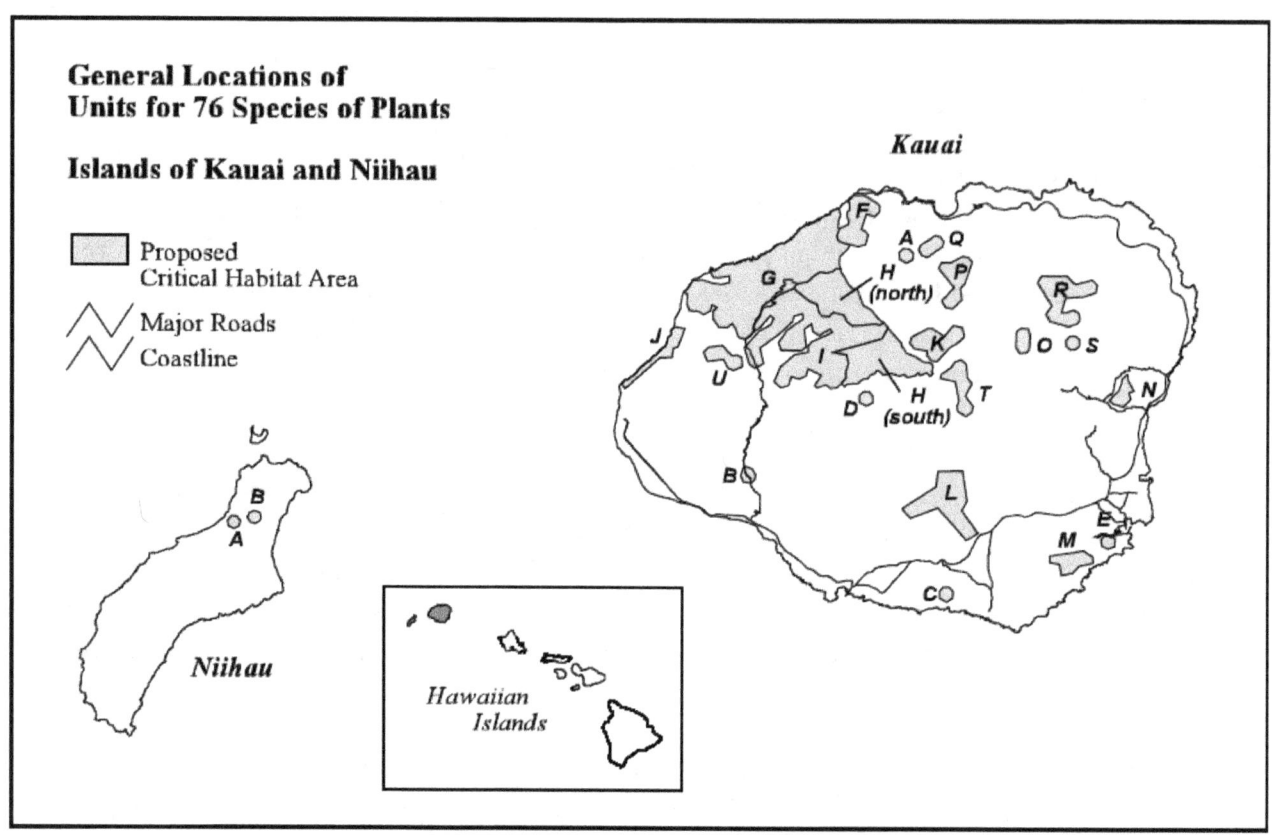

The state owns the largest share (70.9%) of the land proposed as critical habitat while most of the remainder is privately owned (28.8%). Federal land amounts to 0.3%, most of which is managed by the Department of Defense.

Framework and Economic Impacts Considered

The general approach for estimating the economic impacts of the proposed designations used the following analytical concepts and steps, as appropriate:

— Projects, Land Uses and Activities Subject to Analysis

The economic analysis focussed on the "reasonably foreseeable" projects, land uses, and activities that could affect (i.e., *adversely modify*) the 23 proposed critical habitat units. In turn, these were the activities that could be affected by the critical habitat designations. "Reasonably foreseeable" activities are defined as those which are currently authorized, permitted, or funded, or for which proposed plans are currently available to the public.

— Federal Involvement

For the current and planned projects, land uses, and activities that could affect the proposed critical habitat units, the next step in the analysis was to determine Federal involvement. As mentioned above, Federal agencies must consult with FWS whenever an activity they fund, authorize, or carry out may affect designated critical habitat. But activities on non-Federal lands that do not have a *Federal nexus* (i.e., they do not involve Federal funding, a Federal permit, or other Federal actions) are not restricted by critical habitat designations. These activities were not addressed further in the analysis.

— Activities Subject to Consultation in Practice

Historically, not all projects, land uses, and activities that have a *Federal nexus* have been subject to section 7 consultation with FWS (e.g., small grants to farmers to encourage them to voluntarily employ environmentally friendly practices under the guidance of Natural Resources Conservation Service). In view of this practice, the analysis was further confined to those projects, land uses, and activities which are likely to be subject to consultation.

— *Adverse Modification* and *Primary Constituent Elements*

In determining whether there is *adverse modification* to a critical habitat, FWS analyzes the proposed project, land use, or activity, and determines whether it will *adversely modify* the habitat that contains the *primary constituent elements* that are regarded by FWS as being essential for the conservation of the listed species. The *primary constituent elements* are typically described by the type of plant community the plants are growing in, their physical location (e.g., steep rocky cliffs, talus slopes, stream banks), and the elevation. If an action will not *adversely modify* the *primary constituent elements,* either directly or indirectly, FWS reaches a "no *adverse modification"* conclusion, and no further consultation with FWS is necessary. Except for the cost of the consultation, the proposed project, land use, or activity will not be impacted by the critical habitat designation.

In practice, the operation and maintenance of existing features and structures normally would result in a "no *adverse modification"* conclusion because they do not contain, and are not likely to develop, any *primary constituent elements.* Examples are the operation and maintenance of existing buildings, roads, aqueducts, telecommunications equipment, arboreta and gardens, *heiau* (a pre-Christian place of worship or shrine), and other man-made features. In such cases no consultation, or a minimal informal consultation, may be required. Activities falling into this category were not considered further in the analysis.

An equivalent interpretation expressed in the proposed Rule is that existing man-made features and structures that do not contain, and are not likely to develop, *constituent elements* are not included in the critical habitat designation. In effect, these features and structures create unmapped holes that are located within the boundaries of a critical habitat unit, but these holes are are not part of the unit.

—Focus on Incremental Impacts

The analysis evaluated only the incremental economic costs and benefits that are expected to result from the 23 proposed critical habitat designations over and above the economic costs and benefits that would occur under the existing Federal and state protections for the 76 species (see next paragraph). To this end, the analysis compared a "with" critical habitat designation scenario against a "without" critical habitat designation (or "baseline") scenario, and estimated the net change in economic activity that would be attributable to the proposed critical habitat designations. The difference between the two scenarios is the incremental change in economic activity that is likely to result from the 23 proposed critical habitat designations.

Under the baseline "without" critical habitat scenario, the Federal and state governments already protect the 76 plants on Kaua'i and Ni'ihau. For the Federal government, the most significant existing protection derives from the Federal listing of the 76 plants as endangered and threatened species. Because of this listing, section 7 consultations with FWS are already required to ensure that activities are not likely to *jeopardize* the continued existence of these plants. State protections include land-use restrictions for activities in the state Conservation District and specific protections of endangered and threatened plants.

—*Occupied* versus *Unoccupied* Critical Habitat

Typically, an economic analysis for a critical habitat designation focuses on proposed habitat that are *unoccupied* by endangered and threatened species because FWS expects that any potential incremental economic costs and benefits from critical habitat designations will occur predominately on *unoccupied* lands. This reflects the fact that, for lands *occupied* by listed species, section 7 consultations with FWS are already required. There are, however, some cases involving *occupied* lands where ongoing or planned land uses and activities may require re-initiations of consultations that have already been conducted under a species listing, or they may even require new consultations that would not be required with a species listing.

In the Kaua'i and Ni'ihau critical habitat designations, the typical focus on *unoccupied* habitat was not appropriate because all the proposed units are *occupied*, with the possible exception of Alakai Swamp (see Section 2).

—Changes in Consultations, Projects, Land Uses and Activities

For the remaining list of current and planned projects, land uses, and activities that are likely to be subject to consultation in actual practice—and consistent with the focus on incremental impacts—the next step was to estimate incremental changes in the quantity and nature of the consultations and to estimate the changes that were likely to occur in such items as project designs, schedules, land uses, activities, and programs.

It was assumed in the analysis that landowners, Federal agencies and state agencies comply with section 7 of the ESA and other Federal and state laws. Also, the estimates reflected the availability of information which, in many cases, was limited (i.e., the outcome of future consultations will not be known until they occur).

—Economic Effects of the Incremental Changes

The final step in the analysis was to estimate the economic effects of the incremental changes in the consultations, projects, land uses and activities. The kinds of economic costs and benefits that were considered included, but were not limited to, changes in revenues, costs, employment, property values, and the distribution of benefits.

In practice, some types of benefits and costs were impractical to value, largely due to the lack of market prices or existing economic studies on which to base values (e.g., the value of preserving endangered plants).

Economic Impacts

Impact on Economic Activities

For the most part, the 23 critical habitat designations on Kaua'i and Ni'ihau will have modest economic impacts. They are expected to cause little or no increase in the number of section 7 consultations with FWS; few, if any, increases in costs associated with consultations; and few, if any delays in, or modifications to planned projects, land uses and activities. These findings reflect the following:

— Nearly all of the land within the critical habitat units is unsuitable for development as well as for most projects, land uses, and activities. This is due to their remote locations, lack of access, and rugged terrain.

— On Kaua'i, nearly all of this land (98.5%) is within the state Conservation District where state land-use controls severely limit development and most activities.

— Very few of the current and planned projects, land uses, and activities that could affect the proposed critical habitat units have a Federal involvement requiring section 7 consultation with FWS, so they are not restricted by FWS requirements.

— And most of the activities that do have Federal involvement are operation and maintenance of existing facilities and structures, so they would not be impacted by the critical habitat designation.

— For the few projects, land uses, and activities that remain, the incremental economic impacts over and above the economic impacts that would have occurred with the existing species listings and state protections will be small or negligible. This reflects the fact that all of the proposed critical habitat units—with the possible exception of Alakai Swamp—are *occupied,* so they are already subject to consultation to ensure that proposed activities are not likely to *jeopardize* the continued existence of a species.

Based on the above, the critical habitat designation would have little or no economic impact on the following activities:

— Game hunting and control of game mammal populations

— Improvements to and operation of state parks

— Botanical gardens

— Farming operations

— Operation and maintenance of communications, tracking facilities and observatory

— Modifications or additions to communications, tracking facilities and observatory

—Electrical power transmission through existing power lines

—Military exercises on Ni'ihau

—Hurricane recovery efforts, should a hurricane occur

—Residential use of urban lots that extend into a proposed critical habitat unit

—Ecotourism (i.e., privately operated commercial hiking tours).

Impact on Game Hunting

The major issue surrounding the proposed critical habitat designations on Kaua'i concerns the management of game mammal populations (e.g., feral pigs, goats and deer). From an environmental perspective, the major threats to the survival and ultimate recovery of Hawaii's native plants are browsing, digging, and trampling by these ungulates (hoofed mammals), combined with competition from non-native plants that are able to colonize newly disturbed areas more quickly and effectively than can the native plants. According to findings in the proposed Rule, recovery goals for endangered Hawaiian plant species cannot be achieved when these feral ungulates are present in "essential habitat areas." Consistent with this finding, FWS opposes game management that allows or enhances the free ranging of large populations of feral ungulates in areas where there are populations of endangered species. It should be noted that FWS actively supports game hunting opportunities when they do not conflict with the protection of Federally listed species.

While many hunters accept the need to protect limited portions of the native forest from damage by ungulates, the majority of hunters strongly oppose eradicating game mammals from large portions of existing hunting areas. And they fear that designation of critical habitat will lead to a loss of prized hunting areas. Instead, most hunters advocate that game mammal populations continue to be sustained at levels that are sufficient to allow recreational and subsistence hunting in all but possibly a few of the existing hunting units.

DLNR is the state agency responsible for managing game-mammal populations in state Hunting Units. DLNR achieves what they regard as a reasonable balance between sustained-yield recreational hunting and protection of native ecosystems and plants by (1) attempting to keep game mammal populations comparatively low in the nearly pristine areas to minimize harm there, while (2) allowing the populations to increase in the highly degraded areas to provide larger harvests of game mammals for hunters. According to DLNR (but questioned by FWS staff and other biologists), reasonable numbers of game mammals are available to browse on the non-native plants and weeds in degraded areas, thereby helping control the seed reservoir of noxious non-native plants and their spread into other areas. DLNR further notes that eradicating large numbers of game mammals from many of the proposed critical habitat units on Kaua'i would be very expensive.

The issue of game mammal management is a highly divisive and contentious one that has been debated in Hawai'i for many decades. But since the proposed critical habitat units are *occupied* by listed species, with the possible exception of Alakai Swamp, the proposed designations would not change significantly the nature of the debate nor its geographic focus, nor are they likely to result in additional consultations between DLNR and FWS. The impact of the proposed critical habitat designations on hunting would be that they would add weight to the argument that the game mammal populations should be eradicated or reduced substantially in the critical habitat units because they threaten Hawaii's native plants. But, even with the added weight of this argument, DAHI judges the probability to be slight that the state will adopt a policy to eradicate or reduce substantially game mammal populations in affected critical habitat units.

Impact on Property Values

Potential exists for a small decrease in property values for privately-owned agricultural land that is partially located in a critical habitat unit. This decrease in value could occur even though the critical habitat designation would not limit current or planned agricultural uses of the land, and even though no urban development is planned.

The decrease, if any, would involve the <u>speculative</u> component of land value that reflects the potential for eventual urban development; this component typically comprises most of the value of agricultural land in Hawai'i. The decrease could occur if a perception develops that a critical habitat designation will limit eventual urban development of agricultural land. Furthermore, it could be temporary or permanent, depending upon whether the designation will, in fact, restrict urban land uses and/or increase costs for a particular situation. A temporary drop in value, if any, would last until the uncertainty about development restrictions is resolved; early resolution of the uncertainty could entail professional fees. The amount of the decrease could be zero dollars or up to a few thousand dollars per acre, depending upon how buyers and sellers of land react to the critical habitat designations.

Environmental Benefits

If the critical habitat are designated, possible environmental benefits include the survival and recovery of listed plant species, greater biodiversity and healthier ecosystems, the survival and recovery of native wildlife, a reduction in erosion and soil runoff, healthier watersheds, cleaner and healthier streams and nearshore marine environments, and cleaner beaches. However, a monetary value is not estimated for these incremental environmental improvements because of the difficulty of quantifying the magnitude of the changes and the lack of existing economic studies on their value.

PROPOSED DESIGNATION OF 23 CRITICAL HABITAT UNITS

Between 1991 and 1996, a total of 95 plant species historically found on the islands of Kauaʻi and Niʻihau in Hawaiʻi were listed as endangered or threatened species by the Department of the Interior's Fish and Wildlife Service (FWS) under the Endangered Species Act of 1973 (ESA).

When the 95 species were listed, FWS considered critical habitat designation for them, but determined that it was <u>not prudent</u> because it would increase the degree of threat to some species and/or it would not benefit some species. However, these not-prudent determinations, along with 150 others, were challenged in <u>Conservation Council for Hawaii v. Babbitt</u>. On March 9, 1998, the U.S. District Court for the District of Hawaiʻi directed FWS to review the prudency determinations for 245 listed plant species in Hawaiʻi, including 81 of the above 95 species found on Kauaʻi and Niʻihau. The remaining 14 species are known on Kauaʻi and Niʻihau only from historical records (pre-1970), or from undocumented observations, or are no longer extant in the wild. They still occur on other islands in Hawaiʻi, however, and prudency determinations will be made for them in subsequent proposed Rules for those islands.

Upon further consideration, FWS found that critical habitat designation <u>is prudent</u> for 76 of the 81 listed species because the potential benefits of designation essential for their conservation outweigh the risks of designation. For the remaining five of the 81 species, FWS found critical habitat designation to be <u>not prudent</u>: three species because the critical habitat designation would increase the degree of threat from vandalism or collecting, and two species because they are no longer extant in the wild and no genetic material is currently extant. FWS is proposing a total of 23 critical habitat designations for the 76 species.

ROLE OF CRITICAL HABITAT DESIGNATIONS

For all the species that are listed as endangered or threatened, Section 4(b)(2) of the ESA requires FWS to consider critical habitat designation. A critical habitat is a specific geographic area that is determined by FWS to be essential for the conservation of a endangered or threatened species and which may require special management and protection. Critical habitat designation can help focus conservation activities for a listed species by identifying areas that are essential to its conservation, and by heightening the awareness of Federal land management agencies and the public about the importance of the critical habitat.

In addition to its informational role, the *critical habitat designation* may provide protection where significant threats have been identified. This protection derives from ESA section 7, which requires Federal agencies to consult with FWS in order to ensure that activities they fund, authorize, or carry out (i.e., the activities having *"Federal involvement"*) are not likely to destroy or *adversely modify* the *critical habitat*. The ESA regulations define *adverse modification* as any direct or indirect alteration that appreciably diminishes the value of critical habitat for both the survival and recovery of the species.

But even without the critical habitat designation, the *listing of species as endangered or threatened* requires Federal agencies to consult with FWS in order to ensure that activities they fund, authorize, or carry out are not likely to *jeopardize* the continued existence of the *species*. The ESA regulations define *jeopardy* as any action that would appreciably reduce the likelihood of both the survival and recovery of the species.

The designation of critical habitat may include lands that are both *occupied* and *unoccupied* by the species. For geographic areas that are *occupied* by the species, the ESA defines *occupied* critical habitat as areas that contain the physical or biological features that are essential to the conservation of the species and that may require special management considerations or protection.

Unoccupied critical habitat includes those areas which fall outside the geographical area *occupied* by the species, but that may meet the definition of critical habitat upon determination that they are essential for the conservation of the species—that is, they will be needed for its recovery or to stabilize the population. *Unoccupied* lands proposed as critical habitat frequently include areas that were inhabited by the species at some point in the past. In the case of the 23 proposed critical habitat designations on Kaua'i and Ni'ihau, only those units which include Alakai Swamp may be partially *unoccupied*. This is discussed further in Section 2.

Federal agencies will have to consult with FWS regarding any activities they fund, authorize, or carry out that may *adversely modify* critical habitat, regardless of whether the habitat is *occupied* or *unoccupied*. But if the habitat is *occupied* by a listed species, then consultation is already required to ensure that activities are not likely to *jeopardize* the continued existence of the species. Thus, the primary effect of a critical habitat designation is that it requires FWS consultations for activities in areas that are *unoccupied*.

CONSULTATION UNDER SECTION 7 OF THE ESA

As indicated above, section 7(a)(2) of the ESA requires Federal agencies to consult with FWS whenever activities they fund, authorize, or carry out may affect listed species or designated critical habitat. Section 7 consultation with FWS is designed to ensure that current or future Federal actions do not appreciably diminish the value of critical habitat for the survival and recovery of a listed species.

Activities on land owned by individuals, organizations, states, and local and tribal governments require consultation with FWS only if their actions (1) require a Federal permit, license, or other authorization, or (2) involve Federal funding—that is, the activities have a *"Federal nexus."* Section 7 consultation is not required on actions occurring on non-Federal lands when the actions are not Federally funded, authorized, or carried out. Nor is a consultation required on actions that do not affect listed species or their critical habitat.

When consultations concern activities on Federal lands, the relevant Federal agency consults with FWS. When consultations involve an activity proposed by a state or local government or a private entity (the "applicant"), the Federal land management agency with the nexus to the activity (the "action agency") serves as the liaison with FWS. For example, the Army Corps of Engineers is the agency that issues Section 404 permits under the Clean Water Act and so is the action agency. The consultation process may involve both informal consultation and formal consultation with FWS.

Informal section 7 consultation is designed to assist the action agency and the applicant, if any, in identifying and resolving potential conflicts at an early stage in the planning process. Informal consultation consists of informal discussions between FWS and the action agency concerning an action that may affect a listed species or its designated critical habitat. In preparing for an informal consultation, the applicant must compile all the biological, technical, and legal information necessary to analyze the scope of the activity and discuss strategies to avoid, minimize, or otherwise affect impacts to listed species or critical habitat. During the informal consultation, FWS makes advisory recommendations, if appropriate, on ways to minimize or avoid adverse effects. If agreement can be reached, FWS will concur in writing that the action, as revised, is not likely to adversely affect listed species or critical habitat. Informal consultation may be initiated via a phone call or letter from the action agency, or a meeting between the action agency and FWS.

A formal consultation is required if the proposed action is likely to adversely affect listed species or designated critical habitat in ways that cannot be avoided through informal consultation. Formal consultations determine whether a proposed agency action is likely to *jeopardize* the continued existence of a listed species or destroy or *adversely modify* critical habitat. The determination on whether an activity will result in *jeopardy* to a species or *adverse modification* of its critical habitat depends on a number of variables, including the type of project and its size, location and duration. If FWS finds, in their biological opinion, that a proposed agency action is likely to *jeopardize* the continued existence of a listed species and/or destroy or *adversely modify* the critical habitat, FWS may identify reasonable and prudent alternatives designed to avoid such adverse effects to the listed species or critical habitat.

Reasonable and prudent alternatives are defined at 50 CFR 402.02 as alternative actions that can be implemented in a manner consistent with the intended purpose of the action, which are consistent with the scope of the Federal agency's legal authority and jurisdiction, which are economically and technologically feasible, and which FWS believes would avoid *jeopardizing* the species or destruction or *adverse modification* of critical habitat. Reasonable and prudent alternatives can vary from slight project modifications to extensive redesign or relocation of a project. Costs associated with implementing reasonable and prudent alternatives vary accordingly. FWS has indicated, however, that costs attributable to reasonable and prudent alternatives resulting from the section 7 consultation process would normally be associated with a <u>species listing</u> rather than with <u>critical habitat designation</u>, since it is unlikely that FWS would conclude that an action would destroy or *adversely modify* critical habitat without also *jeopardizing* the continued existence of a listed species.

Federal agencies are also required to evaluate their actions with respect to proposed endangered or threatened species, and proposed or designated critical habitat. The regulations implementing the interagency-cooperation provisions of the Act are codified at 50 CFR 402. Section 7(a)(4) of the Act and regulations at 50 CFR 402.10 require Federal agencies to confer with FWS on any action that is likely to *jeopardize* the continued existence of a proposed species or result in destruction or *adverse modification* of proposed critical habitat.

PURPOSE AND APPROACH OF ECONOMIC IMPACT ANALYSIS

Under the ESA regulations, FWS is required to make its decision concerning critical habitat designation on the basis of the best scientific and commercial data available, in addition to considering economic and other relevant impacts of specifying any particular area as critical habitat for a listed species. FWS may exclude an area from critical habitat designation if it determines that the benefits of excluding the area outweigh the benefits of including it unless it determines, based on the best scientific and commercial data available, that this will result in the extinction of the species. The purpose of this report is to identify and analyze the potential economic costs and benefits that could result from the 23 proposed critical habitat designations on Kauaʻi and Niʻihau.

The focus of the analysis is on how the 23 critical habitat designations may affect current and planned land uses and activities on Federally-managed land (including military land) and on state, county, and private lands. For Federally-managed land, critical habitat designation may result in a requirement that the action agency modify its land uses, activities, and other actions in the critical habitat. However, for the state, county, and private lands subject to critical habitat designation, modifications to land uses and activities can be required only when a *Federal nexus* exists (i.e., the activities or land uses of concern involve Federal permits, Federal funding, or other Federal actions). Activities on state, county, and private lands that do not involve a *Federal nexus* are not restricted by critical habitat designation.

To be considered in the economic analysis, activities must be "reasonably foreseeable," which is defined as activities that are currently authorized, permitted, or funded, or for which proposed plans are currently available to the public. This analysis considers all reasonably foreseeable activities on both *occupied* and *unoccupied* lands. Current and future activities that could potentially result in section 7 consultations and/or modifications are considered to be reasonably foreseeable.

The analysis must distinguish between economic impacts caused by the earlier ESA species listings and the additional, or incremental, economic impacts that would be caused by proposed critical habitat designations. The analysis evaluates only the incremental economic costs and benefits that are expected to result from the proposed critical habitat designations over and above the economic effects that are caused by listing the species. Also, if some other existing statute, regulation, or policy limits or prohibits a land use or activity, the economic impacts associated with those limitations or prohibitions are not attributable to critical habitat designation.

Activities of concern on *occupied* lands that result in a *jeopardy* opinion are assumed to result in an *adverse modification* opinion. Thus FWS expects that any impacts or modifications resulting from critical habitat alone (i.e., *adverse modification* without *jeopardy*) will occur only on *unoccupied* lands.

STRUCTURE OF REPORT

The remainder of the report is organized as follows:

Section 2: Species and Habitat Descriptions and Relevant Baseline Information. Provides a physical description of Kaua'i and Ni'ihau, general information on the species, a brief description of the proposed critical habitat units, and regulatory and socio-economic information describing the baseline (that is, the "without critical habitat" scenario).

Section 3: Analytic Framework and Results. Describes the framework and methodology for the analysis, and provides findings of potential incremental costs and benefits resulting from the proposed designations.

INTRODUCTION

In this section, a physical description of Kaua'i and Ni'ihau is provided to help the reader understand the locales of the 76 endangered and threatened species and their 23 proposed critical habitat units. This is followed by a summary of the plants on Kaua'i and Ni'ihau that are listed as endangered and threatened, and a summary of the proposed critical habitat units.

The succeeding subsections provide relevant information about existing regulations and requirements occurring in the baseline; i.e., the "without critical habitat" scenario. Topics covered include: (1) Federal protections for the listed species, (2) state land management affecting development and other activities in the 23 proposed critical habitat units and state protections for endangered and threatened species, and (3) relevant information on how the county of Kaua'i (which is comprised of the islands of Kaua'i and Ni'ihau) manages land.

This is followed by a description of the socioeconomic characteristics of Kaua'i and Ni'ihau, including information on the structure of the economy and where the towns are located. Finally, relevant information is provided on existing and future land-use activities in the 23 critical habitat units under the "without critical habitat" scenario.

PHYSICAL DESCRIPTION OF KAUA'I AND NI'IHAU

The island of Kaua'i is the northernmost and oldest of the eight major Hawaiian Islands. Formed by a single shield volcano, this highly eroded 553-square-mile island has a mountainous interior, deep canyons and valleys that extend from the interior of the island to the coast, and steep ridges and cliffs (see Figure 2-1). Rain falls throughout the upper

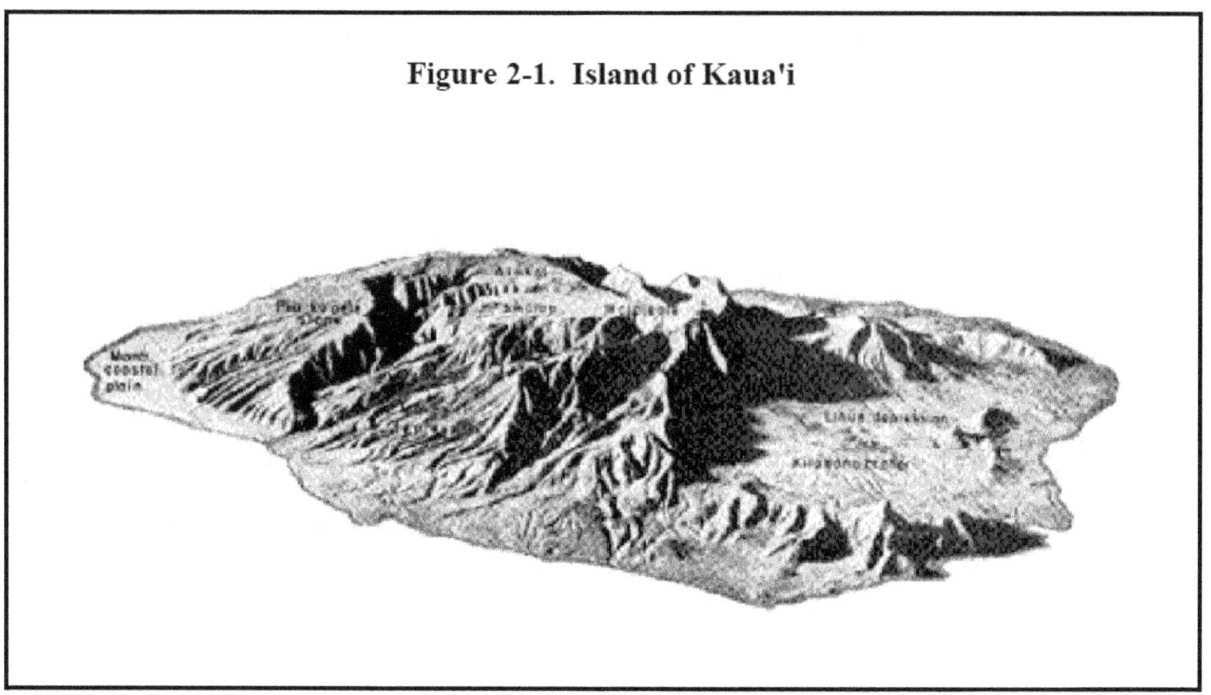

Figure 2-1. Island of Kaua'i

elevations, especially at Mount Waialeale—Kaua'i's second highest point at 5,148 feet in elevation, and one of the wettest spots on earth, where annual rainfall averages 450 inches. The summit plateau constitutes the remains of a huge caldera that is now partially covered by Alakai Swamp, at an elevation of about 4,000 to 4,600 feet. Two of Kaua'i's remarkable natural features are Waimea Canyon and the Na Pali Coast. Waimea Canyon, which cuts deep into the interior of the island, is 14.5 miles long and 2,750 feet deep. The Na Pali Coast was formed by streams that cut deep valleys into the northwestern coast, and by wave action that eroded the shoreline to form precipitous 3,000-foot cliffs.

Because of the age of the island and its relative isolation, levels of floristic diversity and endemism are higher on Kaua'i than on any other island in the Hawaiian archipelago. However, the native vegetation has undergone extreme alterations because of (1) past and present land use (e.g., agriculture) and (2) the intentional and inadvertent introduction of non-native plants and animals. Browsing, digging and trampling by ungulates (pigs, goats, cattle, sheep and deer) have resulted in increased numbers of non-native plants because most of the non-native plants can colonize newly disturbed areas more quickly and effectively than can Hawai'i's native plants. As a result, native forests are now limited to Kaua'i's upper-elevation, moist and wet regions.

Located 17.2 miles to the west of Kaua'i is the slightly younger and much smaller 70 square-mile island of Ni'ihau. Although the island rises to only 1,281 feet, it has precipitous sea cliffs along its eastern coast. Lying in the rain-shadow of Kaua'i, this semi-arid island receives only about 20 to 40 inches of rain per year.

Naturally occurring vegetation on Ni'ihau includes coastal dry shrubland and grassland, dry-cliff plants, lowland dry forest and shrubland, lowland shrubland and grassland, lowland moist forest and shrubland, wetland, and Hawaiian coastal lakes that are abnormally high in salt. One of Niihau's unique natural features is its several intermittent lakes. Ni'ihau's relative isolation and severe environmental conditions have produced a small number of endemic species. Human disturbance—primarily cattle and sheep ranching—has changed the vegetation and hydrologic parameters of the island drastically, leaving little native vegetation.

ENDANGERED AND THREATENED SPECIES

The proposed rule and notice of determination of whether designation of critical habitat is prudent for Kaua'i and Ni'ihau ("the proposed Rule") provides detailed information on the endangered and threatened plant species that were listed by FWS between 1991 and 1996 on the islands of Kaua'i and Ni'ihau. Of the 95 species listed during that period, 14 are known on Kaua'i and Ni'ihau only from historical (pre 1970) records, or from undocumented observations, or are no longer extant in the wild (see Table 1 in the proposed Rule). They still occur on other islands in Hawai'i, however.

Of the remaining 81 species, two (Melicope quadrangularis and Phyllostegia waimeae) are no longer extant in the wild and no genetic material is currently extant. Three other species (Pritchardia aylmer-robinsonii, Pritchardia napaliensis, and Pritchardia viscosa) are not being proposed for critical habitat designation because FWS determined that this would increase the degree of threat from vandalism or collecting, and would provide no benefits.

However, FWS finds that critical habitat designation is prudent for 76 of the species: Adenophorus periens, Alectryon macrococcus, Alsinidendron lychnoides, Alsinidendron viscosum, Bonamia menziesii, Brighamia insignis, Centaurium sabaeoides, Chamaesyce halemanui, Cyanea asarifolia, Cyanea recta, Cyanea remyi, Cyanea undulata, Cyperus trachysanthos, Cyrtandra cyaneoides, Cyrtandra limahuliensis, Delissea rhytidosperma, Delissea rivularis, Delissea undulata, Diellia pallida, Dubautia latifolia, Dubautia pauciflorula, Euphorbia haeleeleana, Exocarpos luteolus, Flueggea neowawraea, Gouania meyenii, Hedyotis cookiana, Hedyotis st.-johnii, Hesperomannia lydgatei, Hibiscadelphus woodii, Hibiscus clayi, Hibiscus waimeae spp. hannerae, Isodendrion laurifolium, Isodendrion longifolium, Kokia Kauai'iensis, Labordia lydgatei, Labordia tinifolia var. wahiawaensis, Lipochaeta fauriei, Lipochaeta micrantha, Lipochaeta waimeaensis, Lobelia Ni'ihauensis, Lysimachia filifolia, Melicope haupensis, Melicope knudsenii, Melicope pallida, Melicope quadrangularis, Munroidendron racemosum, Myrsine linearifolia, Nothocestrum peltatum, Panicum Ni'ihauense, Peucedanum sandwicense, Phyllostegia knudsenii, Phyllostegia wawrana, Phyllostegia waimeae, Plantago princeps, Platanthera holochila, Poa mannii, Poa sandvicensis, Poa siphonoglossa, Pteralyxia Kauai'iensis, Remya Kauai'iensis, Remya montgomeryi, Schiedea apokremnos, Schiedea helleri, Schiedea Kauai'iensis, Schiedea membranaceae, Schiedea nuttallii, Schiedea spergulina var. leiopoda, Schiedea spergulina var. spergulina, Schiedea stellarioides, Sesbania tomentosa, Solanum sandwicense, Spermolepis hawaiiensis, Stenogyne campanulata, Viola helenae, Viola Kauai'iensis var. wahiawaensis, Wilkesia hobdyi, Xylosoma crenatum, and Zanthoxylum hawaiiense.

Most of Kaua'i's endangered and threatened plant species are located in the interior and northwestern portions of the island on steep slopes, precipitous cliffs, valley headwalls, and other regions where unsuitable topography has prevented agricultural development or where inaccessibility has limited encroachment by non-native plants and animals. And, as indicated in Table 3 of the proposed Rule, most of the populations are located on state land and, to a lesser extent, on private land. This same table further indicates that the species populations are small, and 56 of the endangered and threatened species on Kaua'i and Ni'ihau are found only on these two islands.

Text in the proposed Rule further describes each of the endangered or threatened plant species on Kaua'i and Ni'ihau, where their populations are located, the *primary constituent elements* (the physical and biological features) of their critical habitat, and threats to their survival.

PROPOSED CRITICAL HABITAT UNITS

Lands proposed as critical habitat for endangered and threatened plants on Kaua'i and Ni'ihau have been mapped into 23 units, of which 21 units are on Kaua'i (Kaua'i A through Kaua'i U) and two units are on Ni'ihau (Ni'ihau A and Ni'ihau B). As shown in Figure ES-1, the largest units are located in northwestern Kaua'i, with smaller units scattered in other portions of the island. The two small critical habitat units on Ni'ihau are located on the north end of the island.

More detailed maps and information on each critical habitat unit are given in the proposed Rule. The land ownership of each unit and its approximate area are shown in Table 5, and two listings for Kaua'i and Ni'ihau provide the endangered and threatened plant species in each unit. Text provides a brief description of each unit, including the species in the unit, its area, land ownership, natural features, boundaries, and the coordinates of boundary points.

The land area taken up by the 23 proposed critical habitat units amounts to 60,166.14 acres on Kaua'i (about 17% of the entire island) and 470.85 acres on Ni'ihau (about 1% of the entire island), for a total of 60,636.99 acres. Most of the lands are owned by the state:

10

43,004.52 acres, or 70.9% of the lands being proposed. Private lands account for 17,443.01 acres, or 28.8% of the total. Lands owned or leased by the Federal government total 188.89 acres, or 0.3% of the total.

As with the endangered and threatened species, many of the proposed critical habitat units are located on steep slopes, precipitous cliffs, valley headwalls, etc. However, there are exceptions to this generalization: Units E, L, M, O, R and S are located on hills on the west and south sides of Kaua'i; Units L, M and R include some agricultural land at the lower elevations; Units B and C extend beyond gulches to include some agricultural land; Unit J encompasses a beach and agricultural land; and a small amount of Unit N is designated by the state as urban land.

Except for Alakai Swamp (see last paragraph of this subsection), critical habitat units are based on circular areas surrounding every current (post-1970) population of endangered and threatened plants. For multiple populations that are close to one another so that the circles surrounding them overlap, borders were drawn to envelop the circles to create a single large critical habitat unit. Also, boundaries were adjusted to follow significant topological features. In drawing the boundaries for the critical habitat, FWS made an effort to avoid developed areas such as towns, agricultural lands, and other lands that are unlikely to contribute to the conservation of the 76 species.

Each circular area has a radius of 1,924 feet which, according to the proposed Rule, insures enough area to provide for the proper ecological functioning of the habitat immediately supporting the plant. The first 1,760 feet (one-third of a mile) of the radius is consistent with the accuracy of the mapped locations of the plants, and is based on the standard mapping methodology for rare species. The remaining 164 feet (50 meters) correspond with the guidelines in recovery plans for minimum-sized exclosures for rare plants.

With one possible exception (Alakai Swamp, see below), the critical habitat units are regarded as *occupied* by the species. Further, they contain the *primary constituent elements* that are regarded by FWS as being essential to the conservation of the 76 species, and which may require special management consideration or protection. The *primary constituent elements* are described by the general habitat features of the areas in which they currently occur such as the type of plant community the plants are growing in, their physical location (e.g., steep rocky cliffs, talus slopes, stream banks), and the elevation.

Critical habitat can be defined to include areas outside the geographic area currently *occupied* by a species if it is determined that such areas are essential to the conservation of the species. This can include, for example, potentially suitable *unoccupied* habitat that is important to the recovery of the species. However, with the possible exception of the Alakai Swamp (see next paragraph), FWS has not included *unoccupied* habitat in the

11

proposed designations because knowledge is limited about historical ranges of the species (i.e., the geographical areas outside the area presently *occupied* by the species). Also, more detailed information is lacking on the specific physical or biological features essential for the conservation of the species, including information on where the species could be reintroduced successfully.

In contrast to the other proposed critical habitat, Units H, I and T were delineated by including the entire bog and wet forest area of the Alakai Swamp. As a result, <u>portions of these units may include some areas that are *unoccupied*</u> by endangered and threatened species. Within the Alakai Swamp, some plant species grow at the borders of habitat where ecological conditions such as light, moisture, and desiccation change rapidly over short distances. These types of habitat cover comparatively small areas scattered throughout the Alakai Swamp landscape. In addition, individual areas may disappear or may be created over time, depending upon changes in seasonal rainfall or water drainage, or rooting pigs that can alter these edge landscapes and open them to invasive, non-native weeds that can exclude native plants.

FEDERAL PROTECTION OF ENDANGERED AND THREATENED SPECIES

Between 1991 and 1996, the FWS listed 95 plant species on Kaua'i and Ni'ihau as endangered and threatened, including the 76 plants for which the 23 critical habitat designations are being proposed. These species listings require Federal agencies to consult with FWS to ensure that activities they fund, authorize, or carry out are not likely to *jeopardize* the continued existence of the species. Consultation is required with FWS whether or not critical habitat are designated for the species.

At the Federal level, the formal species listing is the most significant aspect of baseline protection because it supersedes other existing protections via its listing provisions. The economic analysis of the 23 proposed critical habitat designations addresses those impacts or potential modifications to activities which are above and beyond the ones that are attributable to the initial species listings of the 76 plants.

STATE LAND MANAGEMENT AND PROTECTION OF NATIVE PLANTS

This subsection discusses state management of public and private lands, with special attention given to permitted and restricted land uses that may affect endangered and threatened species in the 23 proposed critical habitat units. In addition, state protection of endangered and threatened plants and state environmental laws are discussed.

State Land Management

State Districting

All lands in Hawai'i are allocated by the state into one of four districts: Conservation, Agricultural, Urban and Rural. The state, through its Department of Land and Natural Resources (DLNR) and its Board of Land and Natural Resources (the Board) has primary land-management responsibility for activities and development in the Conservation District, while the counties have primary responsibility in the Urban, Rural and Agricultural Districts.

Nearly all (98.5%) of the lands on the island of Kaua'i that are proposed for critical habitat designation are in the state Conservation District; 1.5% are in the Agricultural District; and a few acres are in the Urban District. The entire island of Ni'ihau is in the Agricultural District; none of it is in the Conservation District.

The Conservation District

The purpose of the Conservation District is to conserve, protect and preserve the state's important natural resources through appropriate management in order to promote the long-term sustainability of these natural resources, and to promote public health, safety and welfare (Hawaii Revised Statutes, Sect. 183 C-3). To this end, limited development and commercial activity is allowed in the Conservation District. "Important natural resources" include the watersheds that supply potable water and water for agriculture; natural ecosystems and sanctuaries of native flora and fauna, particularly those which are endangered; forest areas; scenic areas; significant historical, cultural, archaeological, geological, mineral and volcanological features and sites; and other designated unique areas.

Permission is required to use land, construct facilities, or conduct many of the activities in the Conservation District (see below). Permits for routine uses or activities are issued by DLNR, while more complex activities or uses (such as certain construction projects and commercial operations) require formal approval of a Conservation District Use Application (CDUA) by the Board, and often require an approved management plan.

Conservation District Subzones

All land in the Conservation District has been assigned into one of five subzones that reflect a hierarchy of uses from the most restrictive to the most permissive. These subzones are the Protective Subzone (the most restrictive), Limited, Resource, General and Special.

Except for the Special Subzone, all uses and activities that are allowed in a more restrictive subzone in the hierarchy are allowed in the less restrictive subzones. For Kaua'i, 57.4% of the lands proposed for critical habitat designation are in the Protective Subzone, 2.6% are the Limited Subzone, 36.7% are in the Resource Subzone, 0.2% is in the General Subzone, and 1.6% are in a Special Subzone.

Protective Subzone

The Protective Subzone, the most restrictive of the five subzones, was established to "… protect valuable resources in designated areas such as restricted watersheds … plant and wildlife sanctuaries … and other designated natural and unique areas." Correspondingly, lands and waters generally included in this subzone are needed to protect watersheds, water sources, and water supplies; and to preserve the natural ecosystems of native plants and wildlife, particularly endangered species.

No structures, homes, or farm activities are allowed in the Protective Subzone, with two exceptions. First, the land can be used by state and county governments and by non-government entities that serve the public (e.g., the local utility companies) "for public purpose"—i.e., to fulfill mandated government functions for the public benefit such as transportation systems, water systems, and communications systems or recreational facilities. Second, Native Hawaiians owning *kuleana* land may use it for agriculture or single-family residences if their land was used "historically and customarily" for these purposes. (*Kuleana* land is land that was granted to Native-Hawaiian tenants in the mid-1800s.)

Allowed uses (by permit or Board approval) in the Protective Subzone include: replacing or reconstructing an existing structure and some types of accessory structures, habitat improvements for plant and wildlife sanctuaries, Natural Area Reserves, wilderness areas and scenic areas, limited removal of certain trees, and removal of noxious plants from small areas provided that the ground is not disturbed significantly. Limited landscaping is allowed, but is restricted to plants that are endemic or indigenous; alien subspecies are specifically prohibited.

On Kaua'i, 34,521 acres (57.4%) of the lands proposed for critical habitat designation—all of Units K, P and T, and portions of Units A,B, F, G, H, I, L, M, O, Q, R and S—are in the state's Protective Subzone.

Limited Subzone

The Limited Subzone encompasses areas that are potentially dangerous to the public due to possible flooding, soil erosion, *tsunami* (tidal waves), volcanic activity or landslides.

Lands having a general slope of 40% or more are also included in this subzone. The purpose of the Limited Subzone is to limit uses where natural conditions suggest that human activity should be constrained.

In addition to what is permitted in the Protective Subzone, the following activities and uses are allowed in the Limited Subzone by permit or Board approval: accessory structures near existing structures; single-family homes (one per lot) if state and county regulations are followed; agricultural activities; facilities or devices used to control erosion, floods and other hazards; botanical gardens and private parks; landscaping; and removal of noxious plants in areas larger than 10,000 square feet that result in significant ground disturbance.

Just 1,579 acres (2.6%) of the lands proposed for critical habitat designation are in the Limited Subzone. This includes most of Unit E, over half of Units M and N, portions of Unit C, and small amounts of Units F, J and L.

Resource Subzone

The Resource Subzone encompasses lands that are suitable for growing and harvesting commercial timber or other forest products, park land, and land for outdoor recreation (hunting, fishing, hiking, camping and picnicking, etc.). The purpose of the Resource Subzone is to develop properly managed areas to ensure the sustained use of Hawaii's natural resources.

In addition to what is permitted in the Protective and Limited Subzones, the following activities and uses are allowed in the Resource Subzone by permit or Board approval: commercial forestry under an approved management plan, and mining and extraction of any material or natural resource.

On Kaua'i, 22,085 acres (36.7%) of the lands proposed for critical habitat designation (all of Unit U; nearly all of Units A and O; about two-thirds of Units D, F and I; about half of Units B, G, J, N and S; and lesser quantities of H-North, L, Q and R) are in the state's Resource Subzone.

General Subzone

The General Subzone is used to designate open space where special conservation uses may not yet be defined, but where urban uses may be premature. This subzone encompasses lands that may not be adaptable to or needed currently for urban, rural or agricultural use. The General Subzone also includes lands that are suitable for farming, flower gardening, nursery operations, orchards and grazing. Golf courses are not allowed.

In addition to what is permitted in the Protective, Limited and Resource Subzones, facilities necessary for the above-mentioned uses are allowed by permit when these facilities are compatible with the natural physical environment, and the use promotes natural open space and scenic value.

On the island of Kaua'i, only 120 acres (0.2%) of the land proposed for critical habitat designation (small portions of Units E and J) are in the state's General Subzone.

Special Subzones

Special Subzones are designated for educational, recreational and research purposes. These subzones set aside lands possessing unique developmental qualities that complement the natural resources of an area.

On Kaua'i, 940 acres (1.6%) of the lands proposed for critical habitat designation are in Kaua'i's only Special Subzone which is in Unit F. This acreage comprises nearly all of the Limahuli Garden and Preserve which is in Ha'ena on the north shore (see discussion under Unit F).

Additional Management in the Conservation District

In addition to the five subzones in the Conservation District, the state has established further controls by defining other areas they manage within the Conservation District. On Kaua'i, these include the Alakai Wilderness Preserve, two areas that are part of the Natural Area Reserve System, state Forest Reserves, state parks, Hunting Units, and state trails.

Alakai Wilderness Preserve

The purpose of a Wilderness Preserve is to preserve, protect and conserve "all manner of flora and fauna" (Hawaii Revised Statutes, Sect. 183-2 and 183-4). The only such preserve in the state is the 9,939-acre Alakai Wilderness Preserve (the Alakai Swamp) on the summit plateau of Mt. Waialeale between 4,000 and 4,600 feet elevation. It is located in parts of proposed critical habitat Units I, H and T, and spans portions of two subzones: Protective and Resource.

Restrictions include no construction of buildings, roads, or horse trails except under limited conditions; no domesticated animal grazing; no introduction of plants or animals deemed to be objectionable by the Board; no overnight camping except in approved camps; and no mining.

Natural Area Reserves

A Natural Area Reserve (NAR) is based on the concept of protecting ecosystems rather than just a single species, with the goal of preserving and protecting representative samples of Hawaiian biological ecosystems and geological formations (Hawaii Revised Statutes, Sect. 195-5).

Management activities in a NAR include restoring and enhancing existing populations of native plants, removing non-native weeds, and working with local hunters to keep non-native animal numbers low in sensitive areas.

Permitted activities in a NAR include hiking, nature study, and bedroll camping. Game hunting and research or educational activities are allowed by permit. Prohibited activities in a NAR include: improvements or construction; tent camping; vehicles, except on designated roads (no roads are in the Kaua'i NARs); and removing, injuring, killing or introducing plants or wildlife.

Kaua'i has two NARs, both of which are in the Protective Subzone and are located in Unit G on the west side of the island. The Ku'ia NAR (1,636 acres) has two rare ecosystems and examples of lowland dry shrublands and montane wet forests. The Hono O Na Pali NAR (3,150 acres) contains two adjacent mountain valleys terminating in sea cliffs, and has streams, forests, shrublands, grasslands, rare plants and wildlife.

Forest Reserves

State Forest Reserves were first established in Hawaii over a century ago to protect the supply of high-quality water that was being threatened by the destruction of Hawaii's rainforests. The stated purpose of the Forest Reserve is to protect native ecosystems and important watersheds (Hawaii Revised Statutes, Sect. 183-2 and 183-17). Most of Hawaii's state Forest Reserves are in the Resource Subzone. Limited collecting for personal use (e.g., *ti* leaves and bamboo) is allowed by permit, as is limited (no more than $3,000 value per year) commercial harvesting of timber, seedlings, greenery and tree ferns. Commercial forestry operations are allowed only with approval from the Board. Permission is required to reside in a Forest Reserve, hunt in Hunting Units (see below), camp and fish. Land vehicles, mountain bikes, horses, mules and leashed dogs are allowed on designated roads and trails.

Collecting endangered or threatened plants or wildlife is not allowed and, except in the situations described above or with Board approval, no forms of plant or animal life may be removed, injured or killed.

All or portions of Units D, F, G, H, I, J, K, L, O, P, Q, R, S, T and U are located in state Forest Reserves.

State Parks

The State Parks system was established to govern the use and protection of all lands and historical and natural resources in Hawaii's state parks (Hawaii Revised Statutes, Sect. 184-3 and Sect. 184-5).

State parks that are entirely or partially in proposed critical habitat units include:

— Koke'e State Park (4,345 acres) and Waimea Canyon State Park (1,866 acres), both of which are in the mountains and primarily in Unit I and the upper portion of Unit G.

— Na Pali Coast State Park (6,175 acres), which is in Unit G, except for (1) the main camping and hiking areas in Hanakapi'ai Valley and (2) Ka'ahole Valley.

— Polihale State Park (138 acres), a beach park in Unit J on the west side of the island.

For the most part, state parks on Kaua'i are in the Resource Subzone, except for Polihale State Park which is in the Limited Subzone.

Within state parks, approvals are required from the Board to erect communications equipment (such as aerials, antennas and transmitters), vacation cabins (e.g., Koke'e State Park), and concession facilities (e.g., Koke'e State Park). Activities requiring permits include limited camping, lodging (e.g., private and state cabins), hunting, fresh-water fishing, and hiking on certain trails (e.g., beyond Hanakapi'ai Valley in the Na Pali Coast State Park). Uses allowed without a permit from DLNR include camping, limited collecting of renewable products (fruits, berries, flowers, seeds, and pine cones) for personal use; hiking; picnicking; and mountain biking (unless posted signs indicate otherwise).

Hunting

A total of 47 state-managed Hunting Units have been established across the state to control game hunting (Hawaii Administrative Rules, Title 13, Chapters 122 and 123). Kaua'i has ten Hunting Units for hunting feral pigs and goats, black-tailed deer, pheasant (2 species), Francolin (3 species), chukar partridge, Japanese quail, and dove (2 species). All or portions of the proposed critical habitat units are in Hunting Units except for Critical Habitat Units A, C, D, E, M and N. This amounts to about 41,000 acres (33%) of the state-managed Hunting Units on the island.

Hunting is a licensed activity and is restricted within Hunting Units by: bag limits, hunting method (rifle, muzzleloader, bow and arrow, dogs and knives); days allowed (week-ends only), hunting seasons; and hours of the day. Bird game hunting on private land is subject to the same restrictions as it is on state-managed land, while hunting restrictions for the game mammals on private land are set by the landowner. These restrictions are designed to manage the hunting areas, game-mammal populations, and the level of hunting activity to achieve a reasonable balance between (1) recreational benefits for hunters and (2) protection to native ecosystems and endangered and threatened plants.

State Trail and Access Program

The purpose of the state Trail and Access Program is to preserve and perpetuate the integrity, condition, naturalness and beauty of state trails and surrounding areas, and to protect ... environmental resources (Hawai'i Revised Statutes, Sect. 198D-11 and 198D-6).

Activities allowed under this program by permit from DLNR include camping, hunting and fishing. Some trails are designated for commercial activity (e.g., commercial hikes on designated trails), but no commercial activity is permitted on a trail if it will compromise the quality and nature of the experience or cause any damage to the integrity or condition of the trail or the surrounding environment. Prohibited uses include collecting, removing, injuring or killing a plant or animal; and introducing plants or wildlife.

State trails within the proposed critical habitat units are predominantly located in Units G, H and I.

State Protection of Endangered and Threatened Plants

The state has established various laws and administrative rules to protect endangered and threatened plants and their ecosystems. The Administrative Rule "Threatened and Endangered Plants," implements an Act that was specifically designed to conserve, manage, protect and enhance native endangered and threatened plants (Hawaii Revised Statutes, Sect. 195D-3, 195D-4, and 195D-6). Prohibited activities include the taking, selling, delivering, carrying, shipping, transporting, or exporting of any native endangered or threatened plant. However, license holders may sell such plants if the plants are garden-grown.

As discussed above, additional protections of endangered and threatened plants, as well as native plants, are embedded in separate laws governing the state Conservation District, state Forest Reserves, state parks, and designated state trails. In addition to protecting the native plants, the state has laws to protect, conserve and preserve ecosystems in a NAR; "all manner of flora" in the Wilderness Preserve; and native ecosystems and important watersheds in state Forest Reserves.

Limited taking of flora is allowed, but only in state parks and state Forest Reserves, and only if the flora is not endangered or threatened. In state parks, collecting or gathering reasonable quantities of natural renewable products—such as fruits, berries, flowers, seeds, and pine cones—is allowed without a permit for personal use. In Forest Reserves, limited collecting for personal use (e.g., ti leaves and bamboo) and limited commercial harvesting (e.g., timber, seedlings, greenery and tree ferns) is allowed by permit. Commercial forestry operations are allowed only with approval of the Board.

Control of noxious weeds is permitted in the Conservation District as long as no power tools are used and the ground is not disturbed significantly.

State Environmental Assessments (EAs) and Environmental Impact Statements (EISs)

Hawai'i state law calls for efforts to prevent or eliminate damage to the environment and biosphere and to protect endangered species and indigenous plants and animals. To meet this and other goals, Hawai'i's EIS law (Hawaii Revised Statutes 343), which is administered by the state Office of Environmental Quality Control (OEQC), requires that an EA and/or EIS be prepared for many development projects. The law requires that government give systematic consideration to the environmental, social and economic consequences of proposed development projects before granting permits for construction. For impacts on biological resources, OEQC guidelines call for biological surveys, an ecosystem impact analysis, and proposed mitigating measures. The requirements and guidelines apply to development projects in all four state Districts.

Summary of State Management

State protections of endangered and threatened species include: (1) limited development in the Conservation District, its subzones, and other areas they define and manage within the Conservation District; (2) laws specifically addressing the protection of endangered and threatened species; and (3) requirements that an EA and/or EIS address the impact of proposed development projects on biological resources.

Compliance with these State requirements (1) reduces the number of projects that are subject to consultation with FWS, (2) expedites consultations with FWS because much of the information must be generated to comply with the state requirements, and (3) reduces the number of modifications required by FWS to proposed actions and uses.

COUNTY LAND MANAGEMENT

While the state has primary management responsibility for land in the Conservation District, the County of Kaua'i has primary management responsibility for land in the other three state districts: Agricultural, Urban and Rural. Land in the Agricultural District proposed for critical habitat designation amounts to 923.5 acres on Kaua'i (most of Unit C and portions of Units B, J, L, M and R), and 470.9 acres on Ni'ihau (all of Ni'ihau Units A and B).

Crops, livestock and grazing are permitted in the Agricultural District, as are accessory structures and farmhouses. Although land in the Agricultural District is not meant to be urbanized it is, in practice, sometimes used for large-lot subdivisions.

Land in the Urban District proposed for critical habitat designation on Kaua'i amounts to 3.5 acres (Unit N). The urban land includes portions of some residential lots in the Wailua House Lots that extend into a hillside which forms part of this unit.

In addition to its management responsibility for the three state Districts mentioned above, the County of Kaua'i also regulates the development of areas along the coastlines (called Special Management Areas) of Kaua'i and Ni'ihau. Most development in these areas requires a Special Management Area permit from the County.

SOCIOECONOMIC PROFILE OF KAUA'I AND NI'IHAU

To provide context for the discussion of potential economic impacts, this section summarizes economic and demographic information for the County of Kaua'i, which is comprised of Kaua'i, Ni'ihau and a number of small uninhabited islands. The data are summarized in Table 2 1.

Population and Distribution

In 1998, the County of Kaua'i had a population of about 56,600 residents, up 10.6% since the 1990 census. The population amounted to 4.7% of the state population, the smallest of the four counties. Counting visitors, the 1998 de facto population was 72,400 people, up 6.5% since 1990.

Most residents on Kaua'i live in towns located along the perimeter of the island, primarily along the east and south sides of Kaua'i, with smaller populations living in towns on the north shore. There are no towns located on the northwest side of the island (Units F, G and J) or in the mountainous interior. In 1990, only 230 residents, mostly Native Hawaiians, lived on Ni'ihau.

Table 2-1. Socioeconomic Characteristics of the County of Kaua'i

Item	1990	1997	1998	Growth since '90
Resident Population	51,177		56,603	10.6%
Kaua'i Island	50,947			
Ni'ihau Island	230			
de Facto Population	67,963		72,400	6.5%
Visitors				
Annual Visitors	1,286,360		1,040,340	-19.1%
Average Visitor Census	18,200		17,280	-5.1%
Labor				
Civilian Labor Force	25,750		29,050	12.8%
Employed	24,700		26,200	6.1%
Unemployment Rate	4.1%		9.8%	
Jobs, Wage and salary only	25,450		24,900	-2.2%
Construction, mining	1,450		1,050	-27.6%
Manufacturing	900		400	-55.6%
Trans., communication, utilities	2,400		1,600	-33.3%
Trade	7,050		6,800	-3.5%
Finance, insurance, real estate	1,550		1,250	-19.4%
Services and miscellaneous	7,600		9,000	18.4%
Government	3,350		4,000	19.4%
Agriculture	1,150		800	-30.4%
Personal Income				
Total ($ million)	$ 949.8	$ 1,240.5		30.6%
Per capita	$ 18,401	$ 21,941		19.2%
People below poverty level	7.2%	9.9%		
Consumer Price Index—All Urban Consumers, Honolulu	138.10	171.90		24.5%

Source: Department of Business, Economic Development & Tourism. The State Data Book. Annual.

The principal use of the critical habitat units by the general public is recreation, including hiking (all or nearly all of the units), activities within state parks (Units G, I and J), and game hunting (all or substantial portions of Units F, G, H, I, J, K, L, N, O, P, R, S, T, and U).

Economic Overview

The principal economic driving forces for Kaua'i's economy are tourism, agriculture and government.

Tourism

Kaua'i was host to over 1 million visitors in 1998, resulting in an average visitor census of 17,280. However, tourism has declined during the 1990s, due largely to Hurricane Iniki in November 1992 which damaged many hotels, and also due to the prolonged economic recession in Japan. The annual number of visitors and the visitor census were down 19.1% and 5.1%, respectively since 1990. The smaller decline of the visitor census was due to a shift in the mix of visitors, with more American visitors and fewer Japanese: the duration of stay is longer for Americans.

But Kaua'i's visitor industry is on the rebound. Contributing factors include (1) the robust economic growth in California and other western states, and (2) a new generation of aircraft that allows direct flights to California from the short runway on Kaua'i without requiring a refueling stop in Honolulu.

The principal uses by visitors of the proposed critical habitat units are recreation and sightseeing, including hiking and other activities in state parks (Units G, I and J). Also, a small number of visitors engage in game hunting on Kaua'i and Ni'ihau.

Agriculture

For over a century, sugarcane was the economic mainstay of Kaua'i. However, the industry has suffered major contractions since 1990, with some fields being replanted in diversified crops, including coffee, papaya and other fruits, seed corn, flowers and nursery products, and vegetables and melons. Also, some fields have been converted to aquaculture and pasture, and some might be planted in commercial forests. This trend is continuing with one of Kauai's two remaining plantations recently announcing that it will soon close.

Portions of proposed critical habitat Units B, J and L are cultivated in sugarcane by the plantation that announced recently that it will close. Fields in Units B and J could be taken over by the last remaining plantation on Kaua'i.

Portions of Unit C are former sugarcane fields, some of which are now planted in coffee and truck crops and some are used for pasture. On Ni'ihau, the main economic activity is cattle and sheep ranching.

Pacific Missile Range Facility (PMRF)

PMRF—the world's largest instrumented multi-environment range to support surface, subsurface, air and space operations—is a major contributor to the economy, particularly on the west side of the island. Operations vary from small, single-unit exercises up to large, multiple-unit battle-group scenarios. Further development and operations will evolve at PMRF in response to technological advances and defense initiatives. The southern portions of Unit J extends into PMRF, and communication and support sites are located in Unit G and on the border separating Units G and I.

Labor Force and Employment

In 1998, Kaua'i's civilian labor force numbered 29,050 people, up 12.8% since 1990. But employment, which numbers 26,200 people, was up only 6.1%. The lack of economic growth contributed to an unemployment rate of 9.8% in 1998.

While employment increased during the 1990s, the number of wage and salary jobs declined 2.2%. At the same time, the number of self-employed workers and farmers increased. Most of the wage and salary jobs (excluding self-employed workers and farmers) were concentrated in: construction; transportation, communications, and utilities; trade (retail and wholesale); services (hotel, tourism, and health); government; and agriculture. The number of wage and salary jobs declined in all categories except services and government. The declines would appear to be less dramatic if self-employed workers were counted, particularly self-employed farmers.

Personal Income

In 1998, Kaua'i's total personal income and per-capita income were $1.2 million and $21,941, respectively—figures that were up 30.6% and 19.2% from 1990 levels. However, per capita income failed to keep pace with inflation as measured by the Consumer Price Index, which increased 24.5% over this same period.

CURRENT AND FUTURE LAND USES IN THE 23 CRITICAL HABITAT UNITS

Reviewed below are the current and future land uses in the 23 proposed critical habitat units assuming no critical habitat designation (i.e., under the baseline scenario).

Overview

Most of the 23 proposed critical habitat units are unsuitable for development because of their remote locations, lack of access and rugged terrain. Furthermore, state controls severely limit most development. As a result, little development has occurred and very little more is expected. Developments that have taken place are limited largely to improvements in state parks and to communications and tracking facilities.

For most of the units, the predominant use is recreation, such as hiking, game hunting, activities in state parks, etc. Even these uses are limited largely to areas that can be reached by trails.

Types of Development and Land Uses

Existing improvements in the 23 proposed critical habitat units include:
   —Cabins (Unit I and the upper part of Unit G)
   —Irrigation ditch systems (Units G, I, L and R)
   —Park headquarters and a museum (Unit I)
   —Park improvements, such as picnic areas, a picnic pavilion, and restrooms (Units I, J and the upper part of G)
   —Paved roads (Units B, I, J and the upper part of G)
   —Power transmission line (Unit O)
   —Radio towers and appurtenant structures (Units G, J and L)
   —Tracking facilities (Units G, I and J)
   Existing activities include:
   —Botanical gardens (Units C and F)
   —Camping (Units G, I and J)
   —Crop farming and pasture (Units B, C and J)
   —Fishing (Units G, I and J)
   —Game hunting in state Hunting Units (all or portions of Critical Habitat Units B, F, G, H, I, J, K, L, N, O, P, Q, R, S, T and U)
   —Hiking (probably in all units)

Current and Future Uses, by Critical Habitat Unit

Kaua'i A (298 acres)

Approximately 91% of Unit A is in the Resource Subzone of the Conservation District and the remainder is in the Protective Subzone.

No significant development, economic use, or recreational use is known to exist in Unit A. Nor are there any known plans for development, to change a use, or to add new uses.

Kaua'i B (351 acres)

Unit B is bisected by Waimea Canyon Road. The western portion of the property (166 acres, or 47%) is in the state Agricultural District and the remainder is in the Resource Subzone of the Conservation District. The eastern half of Unit B is located in a Hunting Unit.

The land in the Agricultural District is owned by the state and leased to the sugar plantation that is scheduled to close. The fields could be taken over by the last remaining plantation on Kaua'i or made available for another use, such as diversified agriculture, commercial forests, or pasture. Existing improvements include plantation roads and irrigation lines.

Kaua'i C (306 acres)

Approximately 288 acres of Unit C (94%) are in the state Agricultural District, and the remainder is in the Limited Subzone of the Conservation District.

Lawa'i Valley passes through the central part of this unit. Most of the valley is owned by the National Tropical Botanical Garden, which includes McBryde Garden and the Allerton Garden. The National Tropical Botanical Garden is dedicated to conserving tropical plant diversity, particularly rare and endangered species.

The land just outside the valley is owned by A&B Properties. The west side of the valley is planted in coffee, and the east side is used for (1) pasture, and (2) truck crops on fields A&B made available to former sugar workers.

No significant changes in land use are anticipated.

Kaua'i D (308 acres)

Approximately 91% of Unit D is in the Resource Subzone of the Conservation District and the remainder is in the Protective Subzone. Also, all of the land is in the Forest Reserve.

No significant development, economic use, or recreational use is known to exist in this unit. Nor are there any known plans for development, to change a use, or to add new uses.

Kaua'i E (288 acres)

Approximately 84% of this unit is in the Limited Subzone of the Conservation District and the remainder is in the General Subzone.

No significant development, economic use, or recreational use is known to exist in this unit. Nor are there any known plans for development, to change a use, or to add new uses.

Kaua'i F (2,330 acres)

Approximately 43% of this unit is in the Protective Subzone of the Conservation District, 40% is in a Special Subzone, and 17% is in the Resource Subzone; less than half an acre is in the Limited Subzone. Small portions of Unit F are in the Hono o Na Pali Natural Area Reserve and the Na Pali Coast State Park. Also, about one third of this critical habit unit is part of a Hunting Unit.

The dominant feature of Unit F is Limahuli Garden and Preserve, which is located on approximately 1,000 acres of private land in Limahuli Valley in a Special Subzone of the Conservation District. Limahuli Garden is part of the National Tropical Botanical Garden, a privately-managed and privately-supported, non-profit research garden. Its goal is to protect and enhance various habitat of native species living in Limahuli Valley, and to restore important elements of the remnant native forest.

Along the coast of Unit F, Kalalau Trail provides the only land access to the valleys along the Na Pali Coast.

No significant changes in land use are anticipated.

Kaua'i G (15,752 acres)

Encompassing most of the northwest side of the island, Unit G is the largest of the 23 critical habitat units proposed for Kaua'i and Ni'ihau. Approximately 55% of Unit G is in the Protective Subzone and the remainder is in the Resource Subzone. In addition, a portion of Unit G is in a Forest Reserve. Nearly all of this critical habitat unit is designated for hunting.

This unit contains Kaua'i's two Natural Areas Reserves, Ku'ia (1,636 acres) and Hono O Na Pali (3,150 acres), which are protected by the state from development and from nearly all activities other than hiking and game hunting.

Unit G also contains the Na Pali Coast State Park, but excludes portions of Hanakapi'ai Valley and Ka'ahole Valley which are in this park. Hanakapi'ai Valley is the most accessible valley to day-hikers and campers. The park has camping areas and restrooms, and activities are limited to hiking and camping.

Along the shoreline of Unit G, the 11-mile Kalalau Trail provides the only land access to this part of the rugged Na Pali coast. The trail starts at the north end of Unit G and traverses five valleys before ending at Kalalau Beach where the trail is blocked by sheer, fluted *pali* (cliffs).

Unit G also extends *mauka* (toward the mountains) into the higher elevations to contain portions of Koke'e State Park and Waimea State Park. Improvements include a portion of Koke'e Road, cabins, and irrigation ditches that supply water to sugarcane fields in the southwestern corner of the island. Primary activities at the upper elevations of Unit G include lodging, camping, hiking and picnicking.

Finally, four Federal sites are located in Unit G, two of which support the Pacific Missile Range Facility (PMRF). One PMRF support site is located in the southern portion of Unit G on Makaha Ridge at an elevation of 1,500 to 1,800 feet. Facilities include tracking and surveillance radars, telemetry receivers and recorders, a frequency monitoring station, electronic warfare systems, and networked communications systems. The second PMRF support site occupies a portion of the former National Aeronautics and Space Administration (NASA) Tracking Station, which is at an elevation of about 3,700 feet and borders Unit I. Facilities include tracking radars, telemetry, UHF/VHF communications, and command and control systems. The third Federal site is the NASA Koke'e Park Geophysical Observatory in Koke'e Park, which also occupies a portion of the former NASA Tracking Station. The fourth Federal site is the Air Force Koke'e Station located at the northern end of Koke'e State Park at an elevation of about 4,200 feet.

Except for some park improvements and upgrades to the Federal facilities, no significant changes in land use are anticipated.

Kaua'i H (9,750 acres)

Approximately 88% of Unit H is in the Protective Subzone and the remainder is in the Resource Subzone. Most of this unit overlaps with the Alakai Wilderness Preserve; smaller portions of the unit are in Koke'e State Park and in a Forest Reserve. Nearly all of this unit is part of a Hunting Unit.

Activities in Unit H are largely limited to hiking, camping in designated campgrounds, and game hunting.

No significant changes in land use are anticipated.

Kaua'i I (12,629 acres)

Nearly two-thirds of Unit I is in the Resource Subzone of the Conservation District and the remainder is in the Protective Subzone. Portions of this unit overlap with the Koke'e State Park, Waimea Canyon State Park, Alakai Wilderness Preserve, and a Forest Reserve. Most of Unit I is part of a Hunting Unit.

Park facilities and improvements include the park headquarters for Koke'e State Park, the Koke'e Natural History Museum, Koke'e Road, cabins, camping areas, picnic pavilions and picnic areas, restrooms, etc. The NASA Koke'e Park Geophysical Observatory and one of the PMRF tracking stations is on the border of Unit G. Portions of an irrigation ditch system are located in Unit I.

Primary activities include hiking, camping, picnicking, fishing and game hunting.

Except for some park improvements and upgrades to Federal facilities, no significant changes in land use are anticipated.

Kaua'i J (1,245 acres)

About 57% of this unit is in the Resource Subzone, 23% is in the Limited Subzone, and 6% is in the General Subzone. The remaining 14% is in the Agricultural District. A portion of the unit is in a Forest Reserve, and about half is part of a Hunting Unit.

Polihale State Park, which is a beach park, is located entirely within Unit J. Improvements include a campground, a picnic pavilion and picnic area, and restrooms. Activities include beach recreation, fishing, camping, picnicking, etc.

Unit J land in the Agricultural District (172 acres) is inland from Polihale State Park and is owned by the state which leases it to the plantation that is scheduled to close. Improvements include plantation roads and irrigation lines.

The southern end of Unit J extends into PMRF. Known improvements in the unit include a radio tower and a service road.

Planned changes include some park improvements and upgrades to tracking facilities and appurtenant facilities. Also, the sugarcane fields could be taken over by the last remaining sugar plantation on Kaua'i or, more likely, made available for another use such as diversified agriculture, aquaculture, or pasture.

Kaua'i K (2,028 acres)

All of Unit K is in the Protective Subzone. Also, a portion of the unit is in a Forest Reserve, and a small portion of it is part of a Hunting Unit.

Except for hunting and possibly hiking, no significant development, economic use, or recreational use is known to exist in this unit. Nor are there any known plans for development, to change a use, or to add new uses.

Kaua'i L (4,157 acres)

About 67% of this unit is in the Protective Subzone, 30% is in the Resource Subzone, and 0.4% is in the Limited Subzone. The remaining 2% is in the Agricultural District. A portion of the property is in a Forest Reserve, and about 13% of this unit is part of a Hunting Unit..

Unit L improvements in the Conservation District include a radio tower and portions of an irrigation ditch system. The 86 acres of land in the Agricultural District in the southeast corner of this unit are privately owned and have been leased to the sugar plantation that is scheduled to close.

In the Conservation District, no significant changes in land use are anticipated. However, the sugarcane fields will be made available for a new use such as diversified agriculture, commercial forests, or pasture.

Kaua'i M (1,191 acres)

About 52% of this unit is in the Limited Subzone of the Conservation District, 30% is in the Protective Subzone, and 18% is in the Agricultural District. A portion of the 209 acres of land in the Agricultural District are privately owned and were once cultivated in sugarcane. No improvements are evident in the unit other than a 4-wheel-drive road.

No significant changes in land use are anticipated.

Kaua'i N (707 acres)

About 55% of this unit is in the Limited Subzone of the Conservation District and 45% is in the Resource Subzone. In addition, about 3.5 acres (0.5%) are in the Urban District. None of the land is in a Hunting Unit.

The urban land includes portions of house lots that extend into a hillside which forms part of this unit. The property is part of Wailua House Lots, a developed and stable residential community.

No significant changes in land use are anticipated.

Kaua'i O (600 acres)

Nearly all of Unit O (99%) is in the Resource Subzone, and the remainder is in the Protective Subzone. Also, all of this unit is in a Forest Reserve and in a Hunting Unit.

A high-voltage power line and a 4-wheel-drive service road pass through the middle of Unit O.

No significant changes in land use are anticipated.

Kaua'i P (1,758 acres)

All of Unit P is in the Protective Subzone. In addition, portions of it are in a Forest Reserve, and 81% is in a Hunting Unit.

Except for hunting and possibly hiking, no significant development, economic use, or recreational use is known to exist in this unit. Nor are there any known plans for development, to change a use, or to add new uses.

31

Kaua'i Q (627 acres)

About 74% of Unit Q is in the Protective Subzone and 26% is in the Resource Subzone. In addition, portions of Unit Q are in a Forest Reserve, and 11% is in a Hunting Unit.

Except for hunting and possibly hiking, no significant development, economic use, or recreational use is known to exist in this unit. Nor are there any known plans for development, to change a use, or to add new uses.

Kaua'i R (3,004 acres)

About 92% of Unit R is in the Protective Subzone and 8% is in the Resource Subzone. At the eastern edge of the property, about 2.6 acres are in the Agricultural District. Portions of Unit R are located in a Forest Reserve, and 54% is in a Hunting Unit.

The only known improvement on the property is an irrigation ditch system that was built to deliver water to a sugarcane plantation.

No significant changes in land use are anticipated.

Kaua'i S (294 acres)

Nearly 60% of Unit S is in the Resource Subzone and the remainder is in the Protective Subzone. All of this unit is in a Forest Reserve and in a Hunting Unit.

Except for hunting and possibly hiking, no significant development, economic use, or recreational use is known to exist in this unit. Nor are there any known plans for development, to change a use, or to add new uses.

Kaua'i T (1,578 acres)

All of Unit T is in the Protective Subzone. In addition, portions of this unit are in a Forest Reserve and the Alakai Wilderness Preserve, and most of it is in a Hunting Unit.

Except for hunting and possibly hiking, no significant development, economic use, or recreational use is known to exist in this unit. Nor are there any known plans for development, to change a use, or to add new uses.

Kaua'i U (969 acres)

All of Unit U is in the Resource Subzone and in a Hunting Unit. Also, portions of Unit U are in a Forest Reserve.

Except for hunting and possibly hiking, no significant development, economic use, or recreational use is known to exist in this unit. Nor are there any known plans for development, to change a use, or to add new uses.

Ni'ihau A (232 acres) and **Ni'ihau B** (239 acres)

All of Niʻihau A and B, and all of the island of Niʻihau, are in the state Agricultural District. These two units are located at the northern end of the island away from the two settlements in the middle of the island along its western shore. A 4-wheel-drive "trail" passes through the two units.

Ni'ihau is a privately owned island with a small population, most of whom are Native Hawaiians. The primary economic activities are cattle and sheep ranching, commercial game hunting, and military exercises to train downed combat pilots in how to evade capture.

No explicit changes in land use are anticipated in Niʻihau Units A and B. But the owners of the island anticipate additional military contracts that could involve the northern part of the island.

Summary of Anticipated Changes

Assuming the baseline scenario (no critical habitat designation), the only known plans for changes in land use are: (1) upgrades to communications, tracking, and geophysical observatory facilities (Units G, J, I and L); (2) park improvements (Units I, J and the upper part of G); and (3) the recently announced closure of one of the two remaining sugar plantations on Kaua'i (parts of Units B, J and L). Some of the sugarcane fields could be taken over by the last remaining plantation, or they could be made available for another use such as diversified agriculture, aquaculture, commercial forestry, or pasture.

This section gives an overview of the methodology used in the analysis, and the potential incremental economic costs and benefits associated with the proposed critical habitat designations.

METHODOLOGY

The general approach used to estimate the economic impacts of the proposed designations employs the following analytical concepts and steps, as appropriate:

— Projects, Land Uses and Activities Subject to Analysis

The focus of the economic analysis is on the "reasonably foreseeable" projects, land uses, and activities (defined in Section 1) that could affect (i.e., *adversely modify*) the proposed critical habitat units. In turn, these are the activities that may be affected by the critical habitat designations.

For Kaua'i and Ni'ihau, this includes such activities as agriculture, ecotourism, communications and tracking operations, electrical power distribution, botanical gardens, recreation (state parks, hiking, game hunting), and residential use of urban lots.

— *Federal involvement*

For the current and planned projects, land uses, and activities that could affect the proposed critical habitat units, the next step in the analysis is to determine *Federal involvement*. As discussed in Section 1, Federal agencies must consult with FWS whenever an activity they fund, authorize, or carry out may affect designated critical habitat. When consultations concern an activity on Federal lands, the relevant Federal land management agency consults with

34

FWS. When consultations involve an activity proposed by a state or local government or by a private entity, the Federal "action agency" to the activity serves as the liaison with FWS. For example, the Army Corps of Engineers is the agency that issues Section 404 permits under the Clean Water Act and so is the action agency.

Activities on State, county, municipal and private lands that do not have a *Federal nexus (i.e.,* they do not involve Federal funding, a Federal permit, or other Federal actions) are not restricted by critical habitat designations. Therefore, these activities are not addressed further in this analysis.

—Activities Subject to Consultation in Practice

Historically, not all projects, land uses, and activities that have a *Federal nexus* have been subject to section 7 consultation with FWS (e.g., small grants to farmers to encourage them to voluntarily employ environmentally friendly practices under the guidance of Natural Resources Conservation Service). Thus, the analysis is further confined to those projects, land uses, and activities which are, in practice, likely to be subject to consultation. This assessment is based on a review of past consultations, current practices, and the professional judgements of FWS staff and other Federal agency staff.

—*Adverse Modification* and *Primary Constituent Elements*

In determining whether there is *adverse modification* to a critical habitat, FWS analyzes the proposed project, land use, or activity, and determines whether it will *adversely modify* the habitat that contains the *primary constituent elements* that are regarded by FWS as being essential for the conservation of the listed species. As explained in Section 2, the *primary constituent elements* are described by the type of plant community the plants are growing in, their physical location (e.g., steep rocky cliffs, talus slopes, stream banks) and the elevation. If an action will not *adversely modify* the *primary constituent elements,* either directly or indirectly, FWS reaches a "no *adverse modification*" conclusion, and no further consultation with FWS is necessary. Except for the cost of the consultation, the proposed project, land use, or activity will not be impacted by the critical habitat designation.

In practice, the operation and maintenance of existing features and structures normally would result in a "no *adverse modification*" conclusion because they do not contain, and are not likely to develop, any *primary constituent elements.* Examples are the operation and maintenance of existing buildings, roads, aqueducts, telecommunications equipment, arboreta and gardens, *heiau* (a pre-Christian place of worship or shrine), and other man-made features. In such cases no consultation, or a minimal informal consultation, may be required. Activities falling into this category are not considered further in the analysis.

An equivalent interpretation expressed in the proposed Rule is that existing man-made features and structures that do not contain, and are not likely to develop, *constituent elements* are not included in the critical habitat designation. In effect, these features and structures create unmapped holes that are located within the boundaries of a critical habitat unit, but these holes are are not part of the unit.

—Focus on Incremental Impacts

As explained in Section 1, the analysis evaluated only the incremental economic costs and benefits that are expected to result from the proposed critical habitat designations over and above the economic costs and benefits that would occur under the existing Federal and state protections for the 76 species (see next paragraph). To this end, the analysis compared a "with" critical habitat designation scenario against a "without" critical habitat designation (or "baseline") scenario, and estimates the net change in economic activity that would be attributable to the proposed critical habitat designations. The difference between the two scenarios is the incremental change in economic activity that is likely to result from the proposed critical habitat designations.

Under the baseline "without" critical habitat scenario, the Federal and state governments already protect the 76 plants on Kaua'i and Ni'ihau. For the Federal government, the most significant existing protection derives from the Federal listing of the 76 plants as endangered and threatened species. Because of this listing, section 7 consultations with FWS are already required to ensure that activities are not likely to *jeopardize* the continued existence of these plants. State protections include land-use restrictions for activities in the state Conservation District and specific protections of endangered and threatened plants.

—*Occupied* versus *Unoccupied* Critical Habitat

Typically, an economic analysis for a critical habitat designation focuses on proposed habitat that are *unoccupied* by endangered and threatened species because FWS expects that any potential incremental economic costs and benefits from critical habitat designations will occur predominately on *unoccupied* lands. This reflects the fact that, for *occupied* lands, section 7 consultations with FWS are already required to ensure that proposed activities are not likely to *jeopardize* the continued existence of the species. There are, however, some cases involving *occupied* lands where ongoing or planned land uses and activities may require re-initiations of consultations that have already been conducted under a species listing, or they may even require new consultations that would not be required with a species listing.

In the Kaua'i and Ni'ihau critical habitat designations, the typical focus on *unoccupied* habitat is not appropriate because all the proposed units are *occupied*, with the possible exception (see Section 2) of Alakai Swamp (all or most of Units H, I and T).

—Changes in Consultations, Projects, Land Uses and Activities

For the remaining list of current and planned projects, land uses, and activities that are likely to be subject to consultation in actual practice—and consistent with the focus on incremental impacts—the next step is to estimate incremental changes in the quantity and nature of the consultations and to estimate the changes that are likely to occur in such items as project designs, schedules, land uses, activities, and programs.

It is assumed in the analysis that landowners, Federal agencies and state agencies comply with section 7 of the ESA and other Federal and state laws. Also, the estimates reflect the availability of information which, in many cases, is limited (e.g., the outcome of future consultations will not be known until they occur).

—Economic Effects of the Incremental Changes

The final step in the analysis is to estimate the economic effects of the incremental changes in the consultations, projects, land uses and activities. The kinds of economic costs and benefits that are considered include, but are not limited to, changes in revenues, costs, employment, property values, and the distribution of benefits.

In practice, some types of benefits and costs are impractical to value largely due to the lack of market prices or existing economic studies on which to base values (e.g., the value of preserving endangered plants).

The methodology outlined above relies primarily on information provided by FWS, the State of Hawaii's Department of Land and Natural Resources (DLNR), and the consultant, Decision Analysts Hawai'i, Inc. (DAHI). To better understand the concerns of stakeholders, FWS solicited comments and suggestions from the public, other concerned government agencies, the scientific community, industry, and other interested parties concerning aspects of the proposed Rule and the proposed critical habitat units. These comments and suggestions were taken into consideration in conducting the economic analysis. Additional clarifications were obtained from landowners and other parties.

POTENTIAL COSTS AND BENEFITS OF CRITICAL HABITAT DESIGNATIONS

This subsection presents the analysis of incremental economic impacts for those projects, land uses, and activities which could be affected by the designation of the proposed critical habitat on Kaua'i and Ni'ihau.

Overview of Findings

For the most part, the critical habitat designations on Kaua'i and Ni'ihau generally will have modest economic impacts. They are expected to cause little or no increase in the number of section 7 consultations with FWS; few, if any, increases in costs associated with consultations; and few, if any delays in, or modifications to planned projects, land uses and activities. These findings reflect the following:

—Nearly all of the land within the critical habitat units is unsuitable for development as well as for most projects, land uses, and activities. This is due to their remote locations, lack of access, and rugged terrain (see Section 2).

—On Kaua'i, nearly all of this land (98.5%) is within the state Conservation District where state land-use controls severely limit development and most activities (see Section 2).

—Very few of the current and planned projects, land uses, and activities that could affect the proposed critical habitat units have a *Federal involvement* requiring section 7 consultation with FWS, so they are not restricted by FWS requirements.

—And most of the activities that do have *Federal involvement* are operations and maintenance of existing facilities and structures, so they would not be impacted by the critical habitat designation.

—For the few projects, land uses, and activities that remain, the incremental economic impacts over and above the economic impacts that would have occurred with the existing species listings and state protections will be small or negligible. This reflects the fact that all of the proposed critical habitat units are *occupied*, so they are already subject to consultation to ensure that proposed activities are not likely to *jeopardize* the continued existence of a species. The only exception is Alakai Swamp (see Section 2).

Section 7 Consultations

FWS records indicate that, over the past 10 years, no formal consultations have taken place for the 76 listed species on Kaua'i and Ni'ihau. Over the same period, three informal consultations were conducted and, in each case, FWS determined that the proposed actions were not likely to adversely affect the species in question. The three informal consultations were:

—construction of a missile support facility at PMRF by the U.S. Navy (1996)

—activities by the Hawai'i National Guard (1998)

—wildlife damage management to protect Hawaiian Agriculture by the U.S. Department of Agriculture (1998).

In addition, DLNR has held occasional informal consultations with FWS to discuss wildlife restoration and game hunting in the Hunting Units on Kaua'i where listed species are located.

With regard to future consultations affecting the proposed critical habitat on Kaua'i and Ni'ihau, no projects, land uses or activities are known to exist that would require consultation with FWS, other than the occasional informal consultation with DLNR (see Game Hunting below). However, it is reasonable to expect that informal consultations about communications and tracking facilities will take place (see Communications, Tracking and Observatory Facilities below).

Based on consultations during the 1990s, future consultations are expected to number about a half-dozen per decade. These consultations would involve time spent on such efforts as assembling information about the project and the site; preparing for one or more meetings among the applicant, FWS and any other appropriate Federal agencies; the meetings themselves; biological surveys and the associated reports, if any; drafting and responding to letters; and changes to project plans, if any.

However, since all of the proposed critical habitat units are *occupied* by listed species (with the possible exception of Alakai Swamp, see Section 2), consultations would be required, regardless of whether or not critical habitat are designated. Thus, no incremental changes and costs would be attributed to the critical habitat designations above and beyond those which are already attributed to the listing. However, there could be occasional exceptions when consultations would not have been required with a species listing, possibly because a project is located near the boundary of an *occupied* unit.

Game Hunting

The Game-Management Issue

The major issue surrounding the proposed critical habitat designations on Kaua'i concerns the management of game mammal populations (e.g., feral pigs, goats and deer). This is a highly divisive and contentious issue that has been debated in Hawai'i for many decades. The concern does not extend to game birds, however, since FWS currently believes that these birds, and the hunting of them, do not have a significant adverse impact on listed species or their habitat.

As documented in the proposed Rule and various scientific reports and publications, the major threat to the survival and ultimate recovery of Hawaii's native plants comes from ungulates (hoofed mammals), combined with competition from non-native plants. Ungulates feed on succulent seedlings, stems and roots of various palatable native plants. They trample native groundcover plants and uproot seedlings and other low-growing plants. They create openings and sites where invasive non-native plants can become established and spread. Finally, ungulates carry seeds of non-native weedy and invasive plants in and on their bodies, thereby distributing invasive plants to new areas, especially along trails, in and around wallows, and in areas that have been routed up or grazed. Many invasive non-native plants are able to colonize newly disturbed areas more quickly and effectively than can the native plants.

Ungulates cause additional problems which are discussed in the final subsection. In summary, ungulates: (1) contribute to the loss of native wildlife; (2) degrade watersheds and (3) contribute to erosion and soil runoff which, in turn, adversely affects streams, beaches and marine environments.

According to findings in the proposed Rule, recovery goals for endangered Hawaiian plant species cannot be achieved when feral ungulates are present in "essential habitat areas." Ranked in order of importance, the first two of 13 recommended management actions needed to assure the survival and ultimate recovery of Hawaii's endangered plants are: (1) feral ungulate control and (2) non-native plant control. Consistent with this finding, FWS opposes game management that allows or enhances the free ranging of large populations of feral ungulates in areas where there are populations of endangered species. It should be noted that FWS actively supports game hunting opportunities when they do not conflict with the protection of Federally listed species.

Although specific measures to control ungulates are not addressed in the proposed Rule, typical approaches used in a number of biologically important areas across the State include strategic or barrier fencing to prevent or limit the migration of ungulates into designated areas, exclosure fencing surrounding an area and preventing ungulates from entering the protected area, and extensive hunting and trapping to eradicate or nearly eradicate ungulates from protected areas.

While many hunters accept the need to protect limited portions of the native forest from damage by ungulates, the majority of hunters rebel at eradicating game mammals from large portions of existing hunting areas. And they fear that designation of critical habitat will lead to a loss of prized hunting areas as was the case with the court-ordered eradication of sheep and goats from the *palila* critical habitat on the Island of Hawai'i 20 years ago. Instead, most hunters advocate that game mammal populations continue to be sustained at levels that are sufficient to allow recreational and subsistence hunting in all but possibly a few of the existing hunting units. They also see themselves as important contributors to controlling feral ungulate populations at reasonable levels and at little cost to the taxpayer.

Federal Nexus and the Pittman-Robertson Act

The *Federal nexus* for game management on Kaua'i is the Federal funding provided to DLNR by FWS to restore and rehabilitate wildlife habitat and to support wildlife management research. This *Federal nexus* already exists because listed species are present in many of the island's Hunting Units.

The funding is provided as part of the Federal Aid in Wildlife Restoration Act, commonly referred to as the Pittman-Robertson Act. This Act was passed by Congress in 1937 to help restore the nation's wildlife following accumulated damage to forests and grasslands and extensive commercial killing of wildlife. Hawaii's local hunters help fund this program, since revenues for it are derived from an 11% Federal excise tax on the price of sporting arms, ammunition, and archery equipment, and a 10% tax on handguns. Each state's share of these revenues is determined by a formula that considers the total area of the state and the number of licensed hunters in the state. Each state provides matching funds of at least 25% of the program costs from a non-federal source. Also, each state specifies how the funds are to be spent, while FWS serves as an administrative check to insure that the funds are spent in compliance with the Act.

In Hawai'i, the total annual funding amounts to about $1 million per year, of which about $700,000 to $800,000 are Federal funds and about $250,000 are state funds. The island of Kaua'i receives about $187,000 per year for its game-management program plus another $48,000 for non game programs.

Because of the *Federal nexus* (the Pittman-Robertson Act), the potential economic impacts of the proposed critical habitat designations on Kauai's hunting activities are examined below.

Affected Units and Acreage

The 21 proposed critical habitat units on Kaua'i would cover about 41,000 acres of Kauai's ten Hunting Units. This area—which includes all or portions of Units B, F, G, H, I, J, K, L, O, P, Q, R, S, T and U—amounts to about two-thirds of the 60,166 acres of the proposed critical habitat units on the island, and about one-third of the 125,700 acres of Kauai's state-managed Hunting Units. However, many of the hunting areas within the proposed critical habitat units are inaccessible.

Taking into account the additional private lands that are available for game hunting, but which are not managed by DLNR as part of the state's Hunting Units, the 21 proposed critical habitat units on Kaua'i would cover 20% to 25% of the total state and private lands available on the island for game hunting. However, public access to private lands is limited.

Hunting on Kaua'i

Hunting is an important activity for many Kaua'i residents because it provides recreation, subsistence, and a desired lifestyle. Game mammals hunted on the island include feral pigs, goats and black-tailed deer—i.e., the ungulates that are viewed as a threat to the survival and ultimate recovery of Hawaii's native plants. Game birds include pheasant (2 species), Francolin (3 species), chukar partridge, Japanese quail, and dove (2 species).

Statewide, hunting is a significant economic activity, comparable in size to the state's papaya industry. In 1996, 23,000 hunters spent an estimated 258,000 days and about $16.4 million on hunting, of which about $8 million was trip-related and about $8.4 million was for equipment and other expenses (1996 National Survey of Fishing, Hunting, and Wildlife-Associated Recreation). Approximately 70% of their hunting trips were spent hunting game mammals and the remaining trips were for game birds. DLNR data indicate that 8.6% of the game mammal hunting statewide was done on Kaua'i.

To estimate game mammal hunting on Kaua'i, these last two percentages (70% of the hunting trips spent hunting game mammals, of which 8.6% was spent on Kaua'i) are applied to the statewide totals (258,000 days and $16.4 million hunting spent on hunting). The calculations indicate that hunters spent approximately 15,500 days hunting game mammals on Kaua'i in 1996, and they spent about $1 million.

Assuming that these hunters valued their experience at $25 per day (similar in concept to golfers being willing to pay green fees, and based on green fees in Hawai'i), the expenditure in time amounts to $400,000, bringing the total to about $1.4 million as the measure of game mammal hunting on Kaua'i. An estimated $400,000 (30%) of this was spent on hunting in the proposed critical habitat units.

These figures on the value of game hunting should be interpreted as order-of-magnitude estimates, not precise estimates. Also, these figures reflect the recreational value of hunting based on expenditures for supplies and equipment, plus the value of the time the hunters spend on the activity. A valuation of hunting activity based on the value of the meat harvested (i.e., the subsistence value of hunting) would be lower. In effect, hunting is largely a recreational pursuit for which the costs and the value of the time spent are partially offset by the value of the meat harvested.

Finally, hunting on Kaua'i is largely a local activity; no more than 5% to 10% of the hunters come from off-island (based on DLNR estimates).

DLNR Game Management

DLNR is the state agency responsible for managing game-mammal populations in state Hunting Units. However, it must carry out this responsibility in the context of two conflicting mandates: provide for sustained-yield recreational hunting in some of the Hunting Units and protect native ecosystems and plants in other areas.

DLNR achieves what they regard as a reasonable balance between the two mandates by varying their approach according to site conditions (e.g., animal population and food supply), and depending upon whether a particular area is nearly pristine, highly degraded, or somewhere in between these two extremes. The most liberal hunting (e.g., year-round pig hunting) is permitted in nearly pristine areas that have suffered the least environmental damage. This is intended to keep game mammal populations low in these sensitive areas, thereby minimizing harm to native ecosystems and to endangered and threatened plants. However, hunting is not possible in many remote areas that are inaccessible to hunters.

In highly degraded areas where DLNR sees no hope that the vegetation will return to native forest, hunting is restricted in order to sustain larger populations of game mammals (see below for the methods used to restrict hunting). When hunting is restricted, the larger populations allow hunters to harvest more animals each year than would be the case with smaller populations. In addition to the recreational benefits to hunters of having higher game harvests, reasonable numbers of game mammals are available to browse on the non-native plants and weeds, thereby helping control the seed reservoir of noxious non-native plants and their spread into other areas.

The use of game mammals to help control non-native plants and weeds in degraded areas, the use of hunters to help control ungulate populations and their migration into more pristine areas, and the recreational benefits provided to hunters are all accomplished at little cost to the taxpayer.

However, it should be noted that FWS staff and other biologists questions the effectiveness of DLNR's game-management approach in protecting native forests, arguing that so long as large populations of feral ungulates are free to range, they will migrate into areas that are not degraded, possibly because they are fleeing from hunters or searching for better forage than what they can find in degraded game production areas. In turn, their migration into these areas will contribute to the loss of listed plants and the spread of noxious plants.

The methods employed by DLNR to manage game-mammal populations take advantage of the fact that the demand for hunting opportunities exceeds the availability of game mammals. Within each Hunting Unit, DLNR controls the amount of hunting activity by using such restrictions as: bag limits, hunting method (rifle, muzzleloader, bow and arrow, dogs and knives); days allowed (week-ends only), hunting seasons; hours of the day; and for some areas, a limit on the number of daily permits issued. However, hunting activity falls off if hunters' success rates are low, which usually occurs when too many hunters are after too few animals. Also, some of the hunting restrictions are for safety purposes: limiting the number of hunters prevents dangerous overcrowding and risks to both hunters and other recreational users in the area (e.g., hikers and campers).

If the game mammal population becomes too high for an area, DLNR responds by allowing more hunting. But if DLNR believes that the increased hunting does not reduce the population sufficiently—possibly because of difficult access to a remote area—then DLNR would propose that that their staff be used to remove the animals where economically feasible.

To provide guidance for adjusting the controls on hunting activity, DLNR monitors: (1) hunting activity (including the number of hunting trips, game harvests by type of game, and success rates); (2) game populations (using habitat transects, harvest data, hunter reports, and aerial and ground surveys); and (3) vegetation (including the coverage, composition by type of plant, invasion by non-native plants, trends, comparisons with vegetation inside animal exclosures, and impacts to plants from game mammals). But the management of game mammal populations is not an exact science; for example, animal population estimates may be off, populations vary with rainfall and food availability, and animals move from one area to another.

Loss of Hunting Area Due to Critical Habitat Designation

Based on bitter experience, hunters throughout Hawai'i associate critical habitat designation with loss of prized hunting areas. Although a parallel situation does not exist with the proposed critical habitat on Kaua'i and Ni'ihau, the association is based on the *palila* critical habitat on the Island of Hawai'i which is, to date, Hawai'i's only large critical habitat.

In 1975, FWS listed the *palila* (Psittirostra bailleui), a Hawaiian honeycreeper (a bird), as an endangered species. The *palila* depends entirely on the *mamane-naio* ecosystem—a broad band of sparse forest encircling Mauna Kea between about 7,000 and 10,000 feet elevation. In 1977, in an effort to further protect the *palila*, FWS designated the *palila* critical habitat, encompassing about 67,000 acres (105 square miles) of hunting land.

The *palila* were at risk because sheep and goats on Mauna Kea browsed on the *mamane* trees in the *mamane-naio* ecosystem, which was very destructive to the *palila's* habitat. Starting in the late 1940s, the population of game mammals was allowed to increase on the mountain to allow sustained harvest by hunters. Even after the *palila* was listed as endangered and its critical habitat was designated, DLNR continued to manage the feral sheep and goat populations at sustainable levels for hunting, causing continued <u>harm</u> to the *palila's* habitat.

This situation led the Sierra Club Legal Defense Fund to file a lawsuit in Federal court, *Palila v. Hawaii Department of Land and Natural Resources,* to require DLNR to remove the feral sheep and goats from Mauna Kea. The case tested the ESA prohibition on "taking" of any endangered species of fish or wildlife, where "take" is defined as "to harass, <u>harm</u>, pursue, hunt, shoot, wound, kill, trap, capture, or collect, or attempt to engage in any such conduct." At issue was whether modifying a habitat (i.e., in this case sheep browsing on *mamane* trees) may result in "<u>harm</u>" to a species thereby meeting the definition of "taking."

In 1979, a Federal court rendered an opinion in support of the plaintiff. Since studies showed clearly that the sheep and goats were "destroying or altering" the *palila* habitat, the court ordered DLNR to eradicate them from Mauna Kea and this was nearly achieved by 1981. The ruling did not affect the management of pigs on the mountain.

Following this case, FWS regulations defined "harm" to be "an act which actually kills or injures wildlife." The regulations further explain that "[s]uch act may include significant modifications where it actually kills or injures wildlife by significantly impairing essential behavioral patterns, including breeding, feeding, or sheltering."

Even though Hawai'i hunters associate critical habitat designation with eradicating game animals and loss of prized hunting areas, a situation similar to the *palila* critical habitat would not apply to the proposed critical habitat on Kaua'i and Ni'ihau. The reason for this is that the proposed critical habitat on Kaua'i and Ni'ihau are for endangered and threatened <u>plants</u> but not wildlife, while the "taking" provision (which was the basis for the eradication of sheep and goats from the *palila* critical habitat) applies only to listed <u>wildlife</u> and not to plants. And even if the "taking" provision were to apply to plants, it would already be in effect due to the species listing, regardless of the designation of critical habitat.

Impact of Critical Habitat Designations on Kaua'i Hunting

Probability of a Change in Game Management

The impact of the proposed critical habitat designations on Kaua'i hunting would be that they would add weight to the argument that the game mammal populations should be eradicated or reduced substantially in selected areas because they threaten Hawai'i's native plants. In technical terms, this means that the proposed critical habitat designations will increase slightly the <u>probability</u> that DLNR will adopt a new policy on game management: the policy would be to eradicate or reduce the level of game mammal populations substantially in critical habitat units.

As mentioned above, the debate about the management of game mammal populations is a highly divisive and contentious one that has been argued for many decades in Hawai'i—a debate that long preceded the 76 Kaua'i and Ni'ihau species listings. And since the proposed critical habitat units are *occupied*, with the possible exception of Alakai Swamp (see Section 2), critical habitat designations would not change significantly the nature of the debate or its geographic focus.

But, even with the added weight of this argument, DAHI judges that the <u>probability</u> is slight that the state will adopt a policy to eradicate or substantially reduce game mammal populations in the affected critical habitat units—a judgment that reflects discussions with DLNR, others familiar with the subject, and past public comments by hunters over decades. Simply put, the scenario is not regarded as politically realistic: hunters would be up in arms over a proposed reduction in game populations.

In addition to the political problem, there are concerns within DLNR about the initial cost of eradicating large numbers of game mammals from about 41,000 acres dispersed among so many critical habitat units. The most costly to eradicate would be the ungulates in inaccessible areas and the stragglers remaining after hunters lose interest when their success rates drop. DLNR could utilize helicopters at this stage to hunt game, but this is expensive and ineffective in forested areas. Also, snares could be used to trap animals, but DLNR believes that checking them daily is costly, they pose risks to family pets, they are regarded as being inhumane, and they evoke complaints from the public.

Once the game mammal populations are reduced, there are additional concerns within DLNR about the cost of maintaining low populations and of intercepting game mammals that migrate from adjoining non-critical-habitat areas—particularly if hunters are not interested in hunting an area due to low success rates or difficult access.

Impacts on Hunting Conditioned on a Change in Game Management

Assuming, for the sake of illustration, that DLNR were to adopt a policy of reducing game mammal populations substantially in critical habitat units by allowing more hunting followed by using other methods to eradicate stragglers and animals in remote locations, then the following impacts related to hunting could be expected. Initially, the number of hunting trips into the more accessible critical habitat units would increase. But after the populations dropped to low levels, the number of hunting trips into these units would also drop because of low success rates.

Some hunters might continue to hunt in critical habitat units for the wilderness experience. And some might switch to hunting game birds. But most of them would switch to Hunting Units outside the proposed critical habitat units, increasing hunting pressures in these areas even more. And some hunters might choose to hunt less or to not hunt at all, spending their discretionary time and funds instead on other recreational pursuits.

To illustrate the magnitude of the impacts, if the equivalent of about one-third of those who hunt in the proposed critical habitat units were to give up hunting, then hunting activity on Kaua'i could drop by about 10% (one-third of the estimated 30% of hunting activity in the proposed critical habitat units). This translates into a decrease in annual hunting activity of about $140,000 (10% of $1.4 million), which includes the recreational value of the time spent hunting.

For the most part, the $140,000 would be spent by the displaced hunters on other recreational activities, so the net economic impact would be negligible. However, there would be distributional impacts, with some providers of goods and services benefiting at the expense of the stores and service-providers catering to hunters.

Finally, DLNR would probably have to expend more funds to control the game mammal populations in the proposed critical habitat units and to control non-native plants and weeds in degraded areas.

The above outcome would occur only if the state were to adopt a new policy to reduce game mammal populations substantially in critical habitat units. But, as discussed above, the <u>probability</u> of this policy being adopted (and therefore the probability that the above outcome will occur) is slight, even though the proposed critical habitat designations will add weight to the argument that the game mammal populations should be reduced substantially.

The amount of these impacts that would be attributable to the proposed critical habitat designations would reflect the incremental increase in the <u>probability</u> that DLNR would adopt the new game-management policy. While this is not estimated here, it is evident that the amount would be insignificant: it is only an incremental component of a slight probability of the above $140,000 outcome, which would be offset by expenditures elsewhere in the economy.

State Parks

The state parks that are entirely or partially in proposed critical habitat are Koke'e State Park, Waimea Canyon State Park, Na Pali Coast State Park, and Polihale State Park (portions of Units I, J and G). Most of the activity associated with these parks involves operating and maintaining them which is funded by the state.

In Koke'e State Park and Waimea Canyon State Park, planned improvements include: (1) new connecting trails that will link existing trails into a continuous system of trails, (2) interpretive trails near the road to concentrate visiting hikers along a corridor rather than having them venture into the forest, (3) improvements to camping areas, (4) improvements to sewer lines, (5) possibly a new water well, and (6) possibly a reduction in the number of cabins. At Polihale State Park, planned improvements include upgrades to existing facilities and installation of vehicle barriers. In Na Pali Coast State Park, the focus is on better management to restore and protect native plants, protect streams, control invasive plants (e.g., Java plum), reduce illegal camping in areas having native plants, and restore archeological sites. These improvements will be state funded, with no *Federal involvement*.

Under these funding circumstances, there is no *Federal nexus* and therefore no requirement for section 7 consultations with FWS—either for operations and maintenance, or for modifications and additions to the parks facilities.

Depending on congressional action, future Federal funding is possible for land and water conservation in state parks, including funding to help protect habitat of endangered species. However, the resulting *Federal nexus* will not require section 7 consultations or project modifications above and beyond what will occur due to the species listings, because the parks facilities are all located in units that are *occupied* by listed species. Thus little or no economic impact would be attributable to the proposed critical habitat designations.

Botanical Gardens

The National Tropical Botanical Garden (NTBG) is a privately-funded non-profit research organization that operates botanical gardens in Lawa'i Valley and Limahuli Valley (portions of critical habitat Units C and F, respectively). As indicated in Section 2, the NTBG is dedicated to conserving tropical plant diversity, particularly rare and endangered species. The specific goal in Limahuli Garden and Preserve is to protect and enhance various habitat of native species living in the valley, and to restore important elements of the remnant native forest.

Because FWS provides funding for specific research projects and surveys, a *Federal nexus* exists which requires section 7 consultation. But, since the goals of the NTBG are similar to those of the ESA, it is unlikely that the operations of these gardens, or any additions and modifications made to them, would conflict with the ESA.

Also, managed portions of the gardens are regarded as existing man-made features. As such, their operation and maintenance will not be impacted by the critical habitat designation (see "Methodology" above).

Finally, the two botanical gardens, and in particular the preserve portion of Limahuli Garden and Preserve, are located in units that are *occupied* by listed species. Consequently, the proposed critical habitat designations will not trigger section 7 consultations or project modifications above and beyond what will occur due to the species listings.

Thus, little or no economic impact would be attributable to the proposed critical habitat designations.

Farming Operations

Farming operations in the proposed critical habitat units include: (1) coffee growing, truck crops, and pasture in a portion of Unit C; and (2) sugar cultivation in portions of Units B, J and L. The sugar company that is cultivating cane in these units plans to close the plantation, but it is possible that the fields in Unit B, and possibly Unit J, could be farmed by the sole remaining sugar plantation on Kaua'i. The other sugarcane fields are likely to be converted to another crop, cattle grazing, commercial forestry, or aquaculture.

Farming can have a *Federal nexus* if a farmer receives a loan from the Federal Farm Service Agency (FFSA), or receives a small grant from the Natural Resource Conservation Service (NRCS) to voluntarily adopt environmentally friendly practices. Historically, however, the FFSA and NRCS have not consulted with FWS on these loans and grants. As long as there is no change in this practice, it is unlikely that proposed activities in the critical habitat units will require consultations for farm operations.

Communications, Tracking and Observatory Facilities

Radio towers and appurtenant structures are located in Units G, I, J and L; tracking facilities are in Units G and J, and the border separating G and I; and a geophysical observatory is on the border separating Units G and I. The facilities are operated by PMRF, NASA, the U.S. Air Force, and private companies. *Federal involvement* is present in all cases. For PMRF, NASA, and the Air Force, *Federal involvement* is present through land ownership or funding, and for private operations on state land, Federal permits are required from the Federal Communications Commission (FCC).

As noted under "Methodology," the operation and maintenance of existing structures will not be impacted by the proposed critical habitat designations. But planned modifications and additions to facilities will be subject to consultation. Improvements are likely to occur on lands where similar facilities are already present. Since these facilities are located in critical habitat units that are *occupied* by listed species, the proposed critical habitat designations will not cause consultations or project modifications above and beyond what will occur due to the species listings. Thus, little or no economic impact will be attributable to the proposed critical habitat designations

Power Transmission

A high-voltage power line and a 4-wheel-drive service road pass through the middle of Unit O, which is *occupied* by listed species. Since these are existing structures and the main activity associated with them is operations and maintenance, they will not be impacted by the critical habitat designation (see "Methodology" above).

Other Project Development

Unlike some critical habitat in other jurisdictions, no known plans exist for residential, commercial or industrial development in the proposed critical habitat units on Kaua'i and Ni'ihau. Furthermore, proposals for such development would be highly unlikely, with the possible exception of a few homes in suitable areas.

Similarly, the typical kinds of projects, land uses, and activities that would normally trigger section 7 consultations (such as Federally funded highway construction, permits from the Environmental Protection Agency to allow discharges of municipal or industrial wastes, and permits from the Army Corps of Engineers for activities affecting wetlands and streams) are highly unlikely in the proposed critical habitat units.

In fact, no plans of any sort are known to exist for new developments in the proposed critical habitat units on Kaua'i and Ni'ihau. Nevertheless, some unforeseen future projects may arise. If projects are eventually proposed, and *Federal nexuses* apply, then a critical habitat designation can be advantageous or disadvantageous to the project developers, depending upon the circumstances.

The main advantage of having designated critical habitat is afforded to developers who have some flexibility with regard to where they can site their projects. This flexibility may allow a developers to a site project outside critical habitat boundaries, thereby avoiding issues related to endangered and threatened species. This might occur, for example, when siting communications towers or power lines.

But even if there is no flexibility in siting a project, it can still be helpful to developers to know the boundaries of a critical habitat. If a project is located outside the boundaries, then the developer can safely proceed with project planning with little or no risk of facing issues related to listed species. But if a project is inside the critical habitat boundaries, then the developer knows he should have an informal consultation with FWS before proceeding with site plans.

For developers, the main disadvantage of a critical habitat designation—and one that does not pertain to Kaua'i or Ni'ihau—occurs when all of a project, or a portion of it, is proposed for siting within a critical habitat that is *unoccupied* by a listed species. This situation would require a consultation with FWS and possible changes to the project that would not have been necessary with just a species listing. But, as mentioned previously, all of the proposed critical habitat units on Kaua'i and Ni'ihau are *occupied*, with the possible exception of the Alakai Swamp (see Section 2).

Military Exercises, Ni'ihau

The military has a contract with the private owner of the island of Ni'ihau to use the northern part of the island to train downed combat pilots in how to evade capture. On occasion, a pilot may use the trail that passes through Ni'ihau Units A or B. The potential exists for additional military contracts to use portions of the island. Furthermore, *Federal involvement* is present due to the Federal funding.

The owner of the island regards the environmental impact of a pilot traveling on foot through the the two units as negligible, since far greater impacts are caused by grazing cattle and feral pigs in the area. Also, the owner questions the current existence of the listed species in Unit A, *Cyperus trachysanthos*, because it was spotted only in the late 1970s following the two wettest years in the 20th century; its presence is believed by the landowner to have been a temporary phenomenon resulting from the unusual climatic conditions. Also, the species in Unit B, *Brighamia insignis*, is not at risk from training operations because the plant grows on the face of an unstable cliff.

Since the two proposed critical habitat units on Kaua'i are regarded as *occupied* by listed species, their proposed designations will not require consultations or modifications of military exercises above and beyond what will occur due to the species listings. Thus, little or no direct incremental economic impact will be attributable to the proposed critical habitat designations.

Hurricane Recovery

Although damage from hurricanes and other natural disasters is not addressed as a land use in Section 2, a consultation with FWS would be required if financial assistance is sought from the Federal Emergency Management Agency (FEMA) to help residents, businesses and government recover from the occasional hurricane or other natural disaster. In such an emergency, which could affect any and all critical habitat units, FWS procedures are to expedite consultations.

However, since all proposed critical habitat units are *occupied* by listed species, with the possible exception of Alakai Swamp (see Section 2), the critical habitat designations will not cause consultations or project modifications above and beyond those which would occur due to the species listings. Thus, little or no economic impact would be attributable to the proposed critical habitat designations.

Residential Use

The back portions of a few residential lots extend into a hillside and into the fringe of proposed critical habitat Unit N. The properties are part of Wailua House Lots, a developed and stable residential community.

A *Federal nexus* can exist if a homeowner has a Federal housing loan or a loan guarantee. In this situation, the residential use would be regarded by FWS as operations and maintenance of an existing structure, which is an acceptable use within a critical habitat and would not be impacted by the designation.

If a homeowner were to make modifications or additions to a residence using a Federal housing loan or a loan guarantee, this could conceivably be subject to section 7 consultation with FWS. However, any improvements that are made within the confines of a residential lot would not *adversely modify* the *primary constituent elements* that are essential for the conservation of the species. Thus, the modifications or additions would not to be impacted by a critical habitat designation.

Nevertheless, the designation could affect property values somewhat, and impose costs on property owners, particularly those who are selling their property. For a discussion of these impacts, see the following subsection.

Property Values and Costs to Property Owners

General Factors Underlying a Reduction in Property Value

An issue that is commonly raised by private landowners is that their property may lose value because all of it or portions of it are designated critical habitat. They fear that the designation will restrict potential uses of their land or increase their costs, thereby making the property less desirable and reducing its market value.

An illustrative example of this—but one which does not apply to Kaua'i or Ni'ihau—would be a major residential, commercial or industrial project that (1) is located in a portion of designated critical habitat that is *unoccupied* by a listed species but contains the appropriate *primary constituent elements* and (2) has a *Federal nexus*, possibly because the project requires a permit from the Army Corps of Engineers for drainage into a waterway. The developer of the project could experience costs and time delays carrying out section 7 consultations with FWS that are attributable specifically to the designation (and not attributable to the species listings because the project is located in an *unoccupied* portion of the critical habitat), contracting for biological surveys to identify *primary constituent elements*, and changing project plans. When a developer is exposed to such costs and delays, the property becomes less desirable and its market value is reduced.

A reduction in property value need not have a factual basis. Perceptions of the impact of critical habitat designations can result in a temporary loss in property value if landowners or buyers believe that the critical habitat designation will restrict land uses, require modifications to the property, cause project delays, or cause other problems. Such a loss in property value can be incurred for as long as the perceptions persist.

Similarly, uncertainty about the impact of a critical habitat designation can cause a temporary reduction in land value that will continue until clear and correct information is distributed. To reduce the uncertainties, landowners may feel it necessary to retain counsel, land surveyors, biologists, and other specialists to determine the implications of the designation on their property. This can be particularly important for landowners who plan to sell their property and so must address concerns of potential buyers.

The intentional or unintentional misuse of critical habitat designation can also adversely affect property values. For example, opponents to development have been known to take the position in testimony before decision-making bodies that an entire critical habitat, by its very nature, should be preserved and that no development should be allowed within its boundaries—regardless of FWS guidelines about *Federal involvement,* or whether a particular development is proposed for a site that is *unoccupied* and does not contain *primary constituent elements.* To the extent that the opponents are successful, project delays, additional costs, and concerns of investors and buyers can temporarily, or even permanently, lower the value of affected properties.

Potentially Affected Properties

For Kaua'i, concern about a potential reduction in property values is most likely to involve the private lands located in the state's Urban and Agricultural Districts. The specific properties of concern are:

— About 3.5 acres of urban land located on the eastern side of Unit N. The area includes the hillside portions of developed residential lots that are located on the western edge of Wailua House Lots.

— About 288 acres of privately-owned agricultural land in Unit C located to the east and west of Lawa'i Valley. Fields west of the valley are planted in coffee; those east of the valley are used for truck crops and pasture.

— About 86 acres of privately-owned agricultural land in the southeastern portion of Unit L. The land is likely to change from sugarcane to another agricultural use.

— About 209 acres of privately-owned agricultural land that is split between the northern and southern edges of Unit M.

On Ni'ihau, even though the two critical habitat units (Ni'ihau Units A and B) are privately owned and located in the Agricultural District, loss of property value is not likely to be an issue because the island is not subject to development pressures or a significant change in use. Furthermore, the Ni'ihau land market is inactive—the last sale was in 1864 when the family who now owns the island bought it from the Hawaiian monarchy.

For the privately owned cabins in Kaua'i Unit I, concern about property values is not anticipated since these cabins are located on lands that are leased from the State; the leases expire in 2005. Finally, the issue is unlikely to arise with lands located in the state's Conservation District because development and other uses there are already severely limited by access and terrain, as well as by state land-use controls.

Theoretical Impacts on Kaua'i Property Values

For the Kaua'i properties mentioned above (urban use for a portion of Unit N, and agricultural use for portions of Units C, L and M), the proposed critical habitat designations are not expected to restrict current or planned urban and agricultural uses, nor are they expected to expose the landowners to higher costs. The reason for this is that none of the uses on these properties is likely to have a *Federal nexus* that would require section 7 consultations with FWS. And, even if a land use were subject to consultation, it is clearly unlikely that the disturbed portions of farmlands or a disturbed house lot will also contain the *primary constituent elements* for a listed species. Accordingly, in the absence of direct or indirect impacts on the *primary constituent elements,* FWS would have no basis for requesting a change in land use to prevent *adverse modification* to a critical habitat unit.

With no restrictions on current or planned urban and agricultural uses, and no exposure to higher costs, there should be no drop in property values. However, this assumes that all the parties involved with buying and selling the land would also be fully informed about the relevant aspects of the ESA—an assumption that is improbable.

Actual Impacts on Kaua'i Property Values

In practice, modest reductions in property values in some of the critical habitat units are possible. Furthermore, a landowner would attribute these reductions to the fact that a portion of his land has been designated critical habitat since, until the time of the designation, the common perception was that his property had not been impacted by the presence of listed species.

In the case of the urban land (3.5 acres of Unit N), reduced property values, if any, are expected to be modest and temporary, lasting only until uncertainties about the implications of critical habitat designation can be resolved. The lack of a long-term impact on these property values reflects the fact that Wailua House Lots is a fully developed and stable community, and one where the land is developed at its highest and best use—which means that there would be no economic incentive to change the use. The critical habitat designation for this unit would impose no restrictions on continuing the existing urban use.

Reduced property values could be more significant for privately-owned agricultural land that is partially located in a critical habitat unit. The reason for this is that a significant portion of the market value of agricultural land in Hawai'i reflects the speculative component of eventual urban development, even if such development is not planned and, if it does occur, is decades away. For example, the current market value of agricultural land in Hawai'i can exceed $10,000 per acre, while the current agricultural value can be less than $1,000 per acre—most of the difference between the two figures reflects the speculative component of eventual urban development.

If a perception develops that a critical habitat designation will limit eventual urban development of agricultural land (even if no urban project plans exist), then the market value of the land could drop somewhat. This drop could be temporary or permanent, depending upon whether the designation will, in fact, restrict urban land uses and/or increase costs. A temporary drop in value, if any, would last until the uncertainty about development options is resolved. As indicated above, early resolution of the uncertainty could entail professional fees.

Information is insufficient to estimate accurately any temporary or permanent reduction in the value of privately-owned agricultural land in a designated critical habitat. But based on the market value of agricultural land in Hawai'i and on the speculative urban component, the amount could range from zero dollars up to a few thousand dollars per acre, depending upon reactions of buyers and sellers of land.

Costs to Property Owners

A number of the above-mentioned homeowners (Unit N) are likely to investigate the implications of having a portion of their property located within a critical habitat, inquiring as to how the habitat might affect use of their land and its property value. If an owner personally spends an average of one day on such an investigation, then the cost in time could amount to about $200, based on 8 hours valued at $25 per hour. Fees for a professional investigation could be higher: possibly $1,000 based on 6+ hours at $150 per hour.

If a homeowner sells his property, he would have to reveal that a portion of the property is located within a critical habitat, and may want to clarify to potential buyers how the habitat may affect use of the property. In such a case, the landowner may need a document which provides a professional assessment. The cost is estimated at $2,000, based on 12+ hours at $150 per hour.

Similarly, the above-mentioned owners of agricultural land (Units C, L and M), all of which are large landowners, may engage a land-use attorney to evaluate the implications of the critical habitat designation, and draft a short document on permitted and restricted uses, options and recommendations. The cost for such service is estimated at $4,000, based on 20 hours of effort at $200 per hour. Four such landowners could be affected, resulting in a potential total of about $16,000.

Potential for Higher Kaua'i Property Values

Conceivably, some properties might increase in value with a critical habitat designation. For example, a Kaua'i property could become more desirable, and thus more valuable, simply because some people see it as being special or unique because it is officially recognized as a habitat for a number of rare native-Hawaiian plants. Or the whole island might be viewed by many as being a more desirable place to live and visit because of its role in species conservation. A third possibility could be that land near designated critical habitat units could increase in value because this land will not be the focus of species conservation efforts.

However, any increase in value resulting from critical habitat designations is highly speculative and is likely to be insignificant.

Small Businesses

Under the Regulatory Flexibility Act (as amended by the Small Business Regulatory Enforcement Fairness Act (SBREFA) of 1996), whenever a Federal agency is required to publish a notice of rulemaking for any proposed or final Rule, it must prepare and make available for public comment a "regulatory flexibility analysis" that describes the effect of the FWS Rule on small entities (i.e., small businesses, small organizations, and small government jurisdictions). However, no regulatory flexibility analysis is required if the head of an agency certifies that the Rule will not have a significant economic impact on a substantial number of small entities. SBREFA amended the Regulatory Flexibility Act to require Federal agencies to provide a statement of the factual basis for making such a certification.

Small businesses having operations in the proposed critical habitat units include concession operators in Koke'e State Park (Unit I), operators of commercial hiking tours (various units), and small farmers in a portion of Unit C. However, none of these operations is subject to section 7 consultation, nor would they be affected by a critical habitat designation.

But in the unlikely event that DLNR adopts a policy to reduce game mammal populations, only partially due to critical habitat designations, then small businesses that cater to hunters could be adversely affected. Because of less hunting, hunters would divert some of their expenditures from hunting-related stores and services to providers of other goods and services.

Unforeseen Economic Costs

A number of landowners have raised concerns about the unforeseen or unintended economic consequences of critical habitat designations. Their concerns include (1) "creeping federalism," as represented by future expansion of government regulations that ultimately diminish private-property rights, (2) future expansion of state land-use controls emanating from the federal critical habitat designations, (3) eventual government condemnation of private property at depressed land values, (4) costly lawsuits designed to block economic development but justified in terms of protecting critical habitat, etc.

Such concerns can adversely affect property values temporarily or permanently (see above). But future actions identified by these concerns are not part of the proposed designation of critical habitat for Kaua'i and Ni'ihau. Furthermore, they are speculative and too vague for a proper economic impact assessment. But if additional Federal or state regulations are proposed, or if the government proposes to condemn private property, then these actions should be evaluated when they are proposed, and should be based on what is actually proposed.

Ecotourism

Commercial hiking tours, led by professional naturalist guides and featuring Hawai'i's unique ecosystems and endemic plants, are offered in some of the mountainous areas proposed for critical habitat designation. The designations could benefit these operations by providing a marketing dimension that enhances their appeal to visitors. However, this benefit is expected to be slight inasmuch as the area is already regarded as being special—as indicated by the Alakai Wilderness Preserve, the Natural Area Reserves, Forest Reserves, the Limahuli Garden and Preserve, and state parks.

In most if not all cases, FWS prefers that these commercial operations do not feature visits to view endangered and threatened plants since revealing their locations increases the risk that a species may be collected or damaged, or its habitat harmed.

Benefits of Species Preservation

The primary intent of critical habitat designation is to protect areas that are needed to preserve endangered and threatened species. Critical habitat designation can also help educate the unaware landowner or land manager about the importance of protecting habitat of the listed plants on their land.

If these endeavors are successful, environmental benefits expected by FWS staff and other biologists include the survival and recovery of listed plant species, greater biodiversity and healthier ecosystems, and enhanced opportunities for scientific experts to study native plants. In addition, many people derive satisfaction simply from knowing that endangered and threatened species are being saved and that the species will be on earth for future generations to appreciate—even if they may never personally view them. Finally, if the proposed critical habitat designations culminate in the successful recovery of endangered and threatened plant species, then a related benefit will be the reduced regulatory costs associated with establishing and administering the species listings, and the associated critical habitat designations. For the listed species on Kaua'i and Ni'ihau, any reduction in regulatory costs is likely to be modest given the outlook for few consultations (see above).

On a contrary note, some knowledgeable landowners question the contribution that designation of critical habitat will make to the survival and ultimate recovery of listed plant species. They observe that many of these native plants are vulnerable because they are weaker and more fragile than non-native plants, and they grow more slowly. In particular, native plants lack the natural defenses (e.g., thorns, bitter tastes, offensive odors, etc.) to protect themselves from non-native pests (insects, diseases, rats, nematodes, birds, grazing animals, etc.)—a vulnerability which reflects the fact that native plants evolved in isolation in a benign environment. Finally, many of the native plants are unable to compete against aggressive fast-growing exotic plants, particularly when they are stressed, such as during droughts. In the long term, they argue that many listed plants will not be able to survive in the wild, with or without designation of critical habitat.

In any case, a monetary value is not estimated for the incremental benefits related to species preservation because of the difficulty of quantifying these benefits and the lack of existing economic studies on their value. Few studies have been done on the benefits of species preservation and, given the scope of this analysis, no primary research was conducted.

Ethnobotanical Benefits

Closely related to the benefits of preserving endangered and threatened plant species is the benefit of preserving a subset of them that have ethnobotanical uses; that is, they are found in historical plant lore and in the agricultural customs of native Hawaiians. On Kaua'i and Ni'ihau, 14 such plant genera are found in some of the proposed critical habitat units. These are listed in Table 3-1, along with their ethnobotanical uses and the critical habitat unit in which they are located. It should be noted, however, that FWS botanists indi-

Ethnobotanical Use and Plant Genera	Kauai Units																Ni'ihau Unit B	TOTAL Units
	A	D	E	F	G	I	K	L	M	N	O	P	Q	R	T	U	Unit B	Units
Medicinal Use																		
Brighamia			•		•				•								•	4
Chamaesyce					•	•												2
Cyrtandra	•			•			•	•			•	•	•	•	•			9
Hibiscus				•						•								2
Melicope					•	•												2
Nothocestrum					•	•												2
Plantago					•		•					•			•			4
Solanum		•			•	•												3
Wood																		
Alectryon					•	•										•		3
Zanthoxylum						•												1
Food																		
Pritchardia					•													1
Cyanea							•	•			•	•		•	•			6
Dye																		
Kokia					•	•												2
Scent for Barkcloth																		
Dubautia					•	•		•										3
TOTAL Plant Genera	1	1	1	2	10	8	3	3	1	1	2	3	1	2	3	1	1	

Source: Department of the Interior, Fish and Wildlife Service.

cate that further study would be necessary to determine which of the 24 species of these14 plant genera are found on Kaua'i and Ni'ihau have ethnobotanical uses.

Altogether, 17 of the 23 proposed critical habitat units contain plant genera that have ethnobotanical uses, while seven of the units contain none of these genera. As indicated in the table, many of the plant genera are located in Kaua'i Units G and I which, in combination, contain 11 of the 14 plant genera, including six that are found only in these two units.

Designating critical habitat where these plant genera are located could contribute to their survival and recovery. However, no monetary value of the incremental economic contribution is provided because of the difficulty of quantifying this contribution, and the lack of existing economic studies on the benefits of preserving these plants.

Other Environmental Benefits

As discussed in the subsection on Game Hunting, the survival and ultimate recovery of Hawaii's native plants will require controlling feral ungulates inasmuch as ungulates constitute the major threat to listed plants.

It is recognized that ungulates cause additional environmental problems. Their browsing, digging, and trampling contribute to a loss of native habitat which, in turn, contributes to the loss of listed and other native birds, the endangered Hawaiian bat, and snails and insects that are either currently listed or are candidates for listing as endangered or threatened. Also, mosquitoes hatched in pig wallows frequently carry avian malaria and pox that contribute to the decline of native bird populations. Furthermore, certain ungulates (especially sheep and goats) can remove vegetation to such an extent that erosion becomes a major issue. In turn, the loss of vegetation can degrade watersheds, and the soil run-off can increase silt in streams thereby harming aquatic life, create layers of mud on otherwise sandy beaches, and bury near-shore reefs thereby harming marine communities. Adverse impacts are more severe for bays and other protected marine environments that are not flushed by strong ocean currents.

Assuming, for the sake of illustration, that the designation of critical habitat units will eventually result in a significant reduction in the population of ungulates, then the following additional environmental benefits can be expected: (1) enhanced survival of listed and other native wildlife; (2) healthier watersheds; (3) cleaner and healthier streams and nearshore marine environments; and (4) cleaner beaches. However, as discussed in the subsection on Game Hunting, DAHI judges that the probability is slight that the state will adopt a policy to eradicate or substantially reduce game mammal populations in the affected critical habitat units.

A monetary value is not estimated for these incremental environmental improvements because of the difficulty of quantifying the magnitude of the changes and the lack of existing economic studies on their value. Even if they could be estimated, the monetary value would be small so long as the game mammal populations are not changed significantly.

REFERENCES

DeLorme. *Hawaii Atlas & Gazetteer, Topo Maps of the Entire State, Guide to Outdoor Recreation,* Yarmouth, Maine. 1999.

Juvik, J.O. And S. P. Juvik, University of Hawai'i—Hilo, Department of Geography. *Mauna Kea and the Myth of Multiple Use Endangered Species and Mountain Management in Hawai'i.* Mountain Research and Development, Vol. 4, No. 3, pp. 191-202, Hilo, Hawaii. 1984.

The Nature Conservancy of Hawai'i. *Honouliuli Preserve Master Plan* (Draft). Honolulu, Hawai'i. 2000.

R. M. Towill Corporation, Aerial photographs of Kaua'i, October 19, 1992 and November 4, 1992, Honolulu, Hawaii.

State of Hawaii, Department of Business, Economic Development & Tourism. *The State of Hawaii Data Book, 1998, A Statistical Abstract.* Honolulu, Hawai'i. 1998.

State of Hawaii, Hawaii Administrative Rules, Title 13, Chapter 122, *Rules Regulating Game Bird Hunting, Field Trials and Commercial Shooting Preserves.* Department of Land and Natural Resources, Honolulu, Hawai'i. November 1999.

State of Hawaii, Hawaii Administrative Rules, Title 13, Chapter 123, *Rules Regulating Game Mammal Hunting.* Department of Land and Natural Resources, Honolulu, Hawai'i. November 1999.

State of Hawaii, Hawaii Administrative Rules, Title 13, Subtitle 1, Chapter 5, *Conservation District.* Department of Land and Natural Resources, Honolulu, Hawai'i.

State of Hawaii, Hawaii Administrative Rules, Title 13, Subtitle 5, Forestry and Wildlife, Part 1, Forestry, Chapter 107, *Threatened and Endangered Plants.* Department of Land and Natural Resources, Honolulu, Hawai'i. May 15, 1997.

State of Hawaii, Hawaii Administrative Rules, Title 13, Subtitle 6, State Parks, Chapter 146. Department of Land and Natural Resources, Honolulu, Hawai'i. June 8, 1999.

State of Hawaii, Hawaii Administrative Rules, Title 13, Subtitle 5, Forestry and Wildlife, Part 3, Na Ala Hele, Chapter 130, *Rules for Hawaii Statewide Trail and Access Program.* Department of Land and Natural Resources, Honolulu, Hawai'i.

State of Hawaii, Hawaii Administrative Rules, Title 13, Subtitle 5, Forestry and Wildlife, Chapter 104, *Rules Regulating Activities within Forest Reserves.* Department of Land and Natural Resources, Honolulu, Hawai'i. October 1993.

State of Hawaii, Office of Environmental Quality Control. *A Guidebook for the Hawai'i State Environmental Review Process.* Honolulu, Hawai'i. October 1997.

State of Hawaii, Office of Environmental Quality Control. *Definitions.* http://www. state. hi.us/health/oeqc/eioeqc04.html. Honolulu, Hawai'i. February 4, 2000.

State of Hawaii, Office of Environmental Quality Control. *Content Guidelines for Biological Surveys, Ecosystem Impact Analysis.* http://www.state.hi.us /health /oeqc/guidance/ biological. html. Honolulu, Hawai'i. August 11, 2000.

State of Hawaii, Department of Land and Natural Resources. *State Parks on the Island of Kaua'i.* http://www.state.hi.us/dlnr/dsp/kauai.html. Honolulu, Hawai'i. September 2000.

Supreme Court of the United States, Opinion 94-859. *Bruce Babbitt, Secretary of the Interior, et al., Petitioners v. Sweet Home Chapter of Communities for a Great Oregon, et al.* June 29, 1995.

U.S. Department of Agriculture, Soil Conservation Service in cooperation with The University of Hawaii Agricultural Experiment Station. *Soil Survey of Islands of Kauai, Oahu, Maui, Molokai, and Lanai, State of Hawaii.* Washington, D.C. August 1972.

U.S. Department of the Interior, Fish and Wildlife Service, Division of Economics. *1996 National and State Economic Impacts of Wildlife Watching, Based on the 1996 National Survey of Fishing, Hunting and Wildlife-Associated Recreation.* Arlington, Virginia. April 1998.

U.S. Department of the Interior, Fish and Wildlife Service. *1996 National Survey of Fishing, Hunting, and Wildlife-Associated Recreation Hawaii.* FHW/96-HI. March 1998.

U.S. Department of the Interior, Fish and Wildlife Service. *Federal Aid in Wildlife Restoration (Pittman-Robertson).* http://fa.r9.fws.gov/wr/fawr.html. August 28, 2000.

U.S. Department of the Interior, Fish and Wildlife Service. *Palila Recovery Plan.* Honolulu, Hawai'i. January 23, 1978.

U.S. Department of the Interior, Fish and Wildlife Service. *Endangered and Threatened Wildlife and Plants: Determinations of Whether Designation of Critical Habitat is Prudent for 81 Plants and Proposed Designations for 76 Plants from the Islands of Kauai and Niihau, Hawaii; Proposed Rule.* Federal Register, 50 CFR Part 17. November 7, 2000.

U.S. Department of the Interior, Fish and Wildlife Service. *Endangered and Threatened Wildlife and Plants: Proposed Determinations of Whether Designation of Critical Habitat is Prudent for 38 Plan Species from the Hawaiian Islands and Proposed Designations for 50 Plant Species From the Islands of Maui and Kahoolawe, Hawaii.* Federal Register, 50 CFR Part 17. December 18, 2000.

U.S. Department of the Interior, Fish and Wildlife Service, Pacific Region. *Recovery Plan for the Big Island Plant Cluster.* Portland, Oregon. September 1996.

U.S. Department of the Interior, Fish and Wildlife Service, Pacific Region, Department of the Interior. *Recovery Plan for the Multi-Island Plants,* Portland, Oregon. July 1999.

U.S. Department of the Interior, Fish and Wildlife Service, and National Marine Fisheries Service. *Consultation Handbook, Procedures for Conducting Consultation and Conference Activities Under Section 7 of the Endangered Species Act.* (Final) March 1998.

Information was provided in discussions with representatives of the U.S. Fish and Wildlife Service Field Office; the State Department of Land and Natural Resources; A&B Hawaii, Inc.; the National Aeronautics & Space Administration, Koke'e Park Geophysical Observatory; and TEOK Tours, Lihu'e, Kaua'i.